Making Peace

One Woman's
Journey Around
The World

❧

TEXT &
PHOTOGRAPHY BY

Jan Phillips

To Mary,
From one pilgrim to another...
Congratulations on the completion of
your own brave journey toward the Light.

FRIENDSHIP PRESS · NEW YORK

2002

Blessings
Jan Phillips

This book is dedicated to my mother, Mary Marjorie Thesier Phillips, who always encouraged me to love people and follow my heart, and to my father, Leon Dewey, whose spirit guides me gently on my journey.

©1989 by Friendship Press
Editorial Offices:
475 Riverside Drive, Room 772, New York, NY 10115
Distribution Offices:
P.O. Box 37844, Cincinnati, OH 45222-0844

Manufactured in the United States of America
93 92 91 90 89   5 4 3 2 1

The photographs from Thailand were taken jointly by Jan Phillips and Diana Duff, who are credited equally for all photographs in this chapter.

Design ~ Brian Prendergast
Printing ~ Salina Press, Syracuse, New York

Library of Congress Cataloging-in-Publication Data
Phillips, Jan.
    Making peace: one women's journey around the world / text and photography Jan Phillips.
      p.   cm.
    ISBN 0-377-00200-3 : $18.95
    1. Peace – Religious aspects. 2. Phillips, Jan – Journeys.
I. Title.
BL65.P4P55   1989
327.1'72 – dc20   89-28135

TABLE OF CONTENTS

ACKNOWLEDGEMENTS

I want to thank all the generous people everywhere who took me in as one of their own and nourished me in every way, making it possible for this journey to have happened, especially Rita Harper and Akiko Terusaka in Tokyo, the CSJ's in Tsu-shi and Kyoto, the Maryknoll Sisters in Hong Kong, the Zhang family in Beijing, the CFIC Sisters in Quezon City, the Sharma family in New Delhi, the Parikh family in Baroda, Seyril Scochen in Auroville, Charles and Violette Hamati in Cairo, Elana Bairey and Yossi in Haifa, Amos Mund in Berlin, the Baake family in Munster and the Dawson family in London.

I also give thanks to my friend, Alethea Connolly, for being the solid ground beneath my feet and encouraging me to keep writing when flight was so attractive. To Susie Gaynes, Amy Bartell and Karen Elias for inspiring me with your energy and rubbing my head when I needed help. To my family, for believing in my dreams and loving me so powerfully. To Margaret Lalor for encouraging me early on to live passionately. To Grandma Thesier and Grandma Phillips, thank you for staying well while I was gone, so I could come home to you and share the wonders of this trip. Many thanks to Catherine Rowe for your attentive and loving support while I was en route, and to Diana Duff, Sandie Bowman and Mom for joining me and playing along the way. And to Patricia O'Connor, thank you for doing it first so I knew it was possible to go around the world by myself.

You have all contributed greatly to my life and I love each of you so very much. Thank you!

Jan Phillips
– September, 1989

Mother Teresa's orphanage, Calcutta, India.

In the spring of 1983 I left Syracuse, New York, on a journey for peace around the world. My backpack was loaded with cameras and film and a slideshow about the U.S. disarmament movement. As a photographer and activist for social justice, I'd spent many years chronicling the signs of an evolving global consciousness. Now I wanted to share those images and pass on the spirit of courage and change.

In order to create a culture of peace, a culture that reflects our reverence for life, we need stories and symbols that heal and guide, that help us remember we are part of a whole. It's hard, in a society bent on profit, to remember what life is really for. Harder still to connect with one another when most things serve to keep us separate. But stories help. Pictures help. And every contact with a lover of life brings us one step closer to loving our own.

My journey was a search for those images and stories, an attempt to discover and reveal our oneness around the globe. It led to events that changed my life, from the day I arrived in Tokyo, Japan.

In response to an interview in a Japanese newspaper, I was invited to speak in several cities, including Nagasaki where I had the chance to meet with a group of *hibakusha,* survivors of the atomic bomb.

Mr. Terumasa Matsunaga, a deputy director of the Nagasaki Association for the Promotion of Peace, had invited me to a gathering of the local *hibakusha*. They were going to watch the premiere of a Japanese film, one which included recently released American military footage of the Nagasaki bombing. Following that, I was scheduled to show slides and talk about the U.S. peace movement.

As the lights went out, we sat in the back, huddled close so Mr. Matsunaga could translate quietly. The film began with a slow pan of the Peace Park, Nagasaki's memorial to the bomb's victims. Colorful flowers and paper cranes filled the frame until the lens widened for an aerial view. From the sky it looked like any city, glittering gold in the afternoon light. Mr. Matsunaga was proudly describing his native city and everything was fine till the film took us back forty years. With a sudden cut, the footage changed and we were viewing Nagasaki from a U.S. plane on August 9, 1945.

We watched the bomb drop. Watched the deadly cloud devour the city. And then from the ground we watched what followed. Mr. Matsunaga, his calm voice silenced, collapsed into tears by my side. The survivors in front of us never moved. Frozen in time, they stared ahead, watching themselves on the silver screen stumbling through the rubble of charred corpses. Dazed and burned, they were calling for families they would never find. Gasps and quiet sobs filled the room while we witnessed the re-run of a nuclear holocaust. When it was over, no one moved. No one turned on a light. We just sat there together in the dark, with such pain around us.

After a while, the lights came on and I was introduced. When I stood before them I started to cry, but they urged me on. We watched slides of a million people marching through New York for nuclear disarmament, including the delegation from Japan that had flown in to participate. When they saw the photo of an aging Buddhist monk, his wheelchair lifted above the crowds by a group of young monks in saffron robes, they called out his name with great respect. Watching the faces of young and old, people of many cultures and colors gathered together for global peace, they cried again, this time for joy. They said they never knew so many people cared.

I had a tape recorder and asked if any of them would speak so I could take their messages to other people. One by one they talked through their tears of the horrors they'd lived with for forty years and of the hope it gave them to see so many people speaking out against war. Into the microphone, over and over, they spoke the same words:

"We Must Never Let This Terrible Thing Happen Again."

It was that memory that kept me moving through the next eighteen months, through fifteen countries, through my many fearful and fragile moments.

In the Philippines I watched the drama of a peaceful revolution as the people claimed their right to survive. I pondered peace from the inside out at a Buddhist retreat in the Japanese Alps. For three weeks I lived in a Gandhian ashram with a man who left his family at age fourteen to live with the Mahatma until the night of his death. Through mainland

China to the Himalayas, India to the Middle East, I walked through the landscapes of hope and human kindness. I was cared for and nourished by Arabs and Israelis, Hindus and Muslims, communists and capitalists, Christians and atheists. I found no barriers at the level of the heart. People who shared their experiences and feelings, no matter what their perspective, enriched my life. As we gathered in churches and schools, ashrams and temples, kitchens and boardrooms and bamboo huts, we sang and talked, cried and prayed, remembering ourselves as a family again.

This book is a collection of those memories. It's a story of people making choices, making change. A story of ordinary heroes whose work for peace finds no applause, is rarely noticed, can never be measured. For it is only the future that can measure our gains.

2

BELOW: Peace activists at a silent vigil in Syracuse, New York, commemorating the bombing of Hiroshima and Nagasaki.

FACING PAGE: Buddhist monks from Japan pray for peace during June 12 rally.

When I stepped off the train my first day in Tokyo, these schoolchildren were all standing in line being very quiet and well behaved. As soon as they saw me, dozens of them rushed over to give their little peace signs, though none knew who I was or why I was there. It felt like a blessing on the beginning of a long and remarkable journey.

WELCOME TO TOKYO

I arrived in Japan late at night and by the time I cleared customs, I was so exhausted I could hardly lift my sixty-pound backpack. Having previously traveled in Europe, I was confident that I could find my way by simply reading the signs to different cities. What hadn't occurred to me was that all the signs would be written in Japanese characters.

Dragging my pack from sign to sign, I searched for a symbol that looked like Tokyo. Finally, I cried out in despair, "Which way to Tokyo?" and the crowds stopped short at this unusual display of emotion. An older gentleman came up to me and I showed him the address of a friend of a friend who had offered to put me up for a few days. He led me to the train I needed, but warned that I would have to change trains twice to get to her house.

A bigger nightmare than this I could hardly imagine. Not only did I not know where I was going, I could not pronounce the name of the town in a way that was understandable to any Japanese person. I managed to make the first train change with the help of a young student, but by this time it was midnight and the only other riders were a few drunken businessmen in three-piece suits trying to help each other stand up. We rode and rode till the end of the line – me, frozen in culture shock, they having the time of their lives. Thinking there would be another train to catch, I gathered my belongings and jumped down from the coach when it eased into a station a half-hour beyond Tokyo. What a surprise to find an empty terminal and no more trains.

Within moments, the people vanished and I was standing alone on a dark, crisp night in what felt to me like the Twilight Zone. All I could hear was the loud panicky beat of my heart, th-thump, th-thump. I hoisted my pack onto my back and took off down the hill, finding a pub a few blocks away. Thrilled at the signs of light and life, I walked in, sat down and ordered a beer. Then I cried for the next twenty mintues. All I wanted was to be back home again. When I finally collected myself, I showed the address to some people at the bar and asked if any of them knew where it was. As it turned out, I wasn't too far from my destination, so the bartender called a cab and I was there in an hour.

Anxious to begin the peace pilgrimage I had been working toward for two years, I started the next day to put the gears in motion. I called the *Mainichi*, Japan's English-language newspaper and asked for the features editor. When I explained that I was an American photographer traveling with a slideshow about the U.S. Peace Movement and that I was trying to connect with groups to talk about the possibilities of making peace in the world, he sent over a reporter and photographer. The next day the paper published a feature story and printed my phone number for groups who wanted to see *Focus on Peace* and have me speak. Within three days, I was booked solid for five weeks.

I had no idea before I started how this journey for peace would take shape, but it soon took on a life of its own, and Japan turned out to be a perfect launching pad for an incredible inquiry into possibility.

FIRE IN MY EYES:
MEMORIES OF AN A-BOMB SURVIVOR

I was invited to Nagasaki by Mr. Terumasa Matsunaga, the deputy director for the Nagasaki Association for the Promotion of Peace. He had arranged for an afternoon meeting with the Hibakusha (A-bomb survivors) and a morning interview with Tsuyo Kataoka, a survivor who was willing to share her story with me. These are her words, graciously interpreted by Mr. Matsunaga:

At the age of twenty-four I was working in the Mitsubishi Munitions Factory and living with my family. On the afternoon of August 9, my co-workers and I were resting outside the building when we heard a great explosion. My eyes began to burn like they were on fire and from nowhere came a force that threw me very far. When I regained my consciousness, there were few people around me. We were close to the Urakami River, so I made my way there along with many others. What I saw at the river was the most horrible sight I can remember.

The river water was stained red and filled with people who were washing out their wounds. The riverbank was crowded with people groaning and calling out for their families. They were panting for water and a huge thirst overcame us all. In order to cross the river, I had to walk over the wounded since we were all so crowded together. I was nearly naked and sick with the smell of my burning body.

Finally, I made it to where my house was once, but nothing was left. Everything had been blown away, including the trees and buildings that once surrounded us. I cried out for my family members and was so happy to see my mother who had survived. Right after I found her, I lost my eyesight, so my mother, who was sixty-nine, had to care for me. Two days later, I lost my hearing.

We wandered around for days looking for shelter until we ended up at the St. Francis Hospital. Though the hospital was nearly destroyed, we found a place to lay our mat. Soon after we were there, a terrible thing happened. It began to rain very hard and the wind was so strong it blew it in on me. The rain was very oily and dark and soon my whole body was covered with it. The smell and touch of that was so terrible I will never forget it.

For the next few weeks, my mother tried to nurse me since I only received treatment once since I had been there. There were very few doctors to treat the hundreds of people who were crying out for help. My wounds were not healing and once, while my mother was gone, flies gathered round the open sores and maggots hatched in the wounds. It was very difficult for my mother to tend to this. She prayed very hard and went to church as often as she could.

On September 20, my eyesight came back like a miracle. I was so happy to see again, though the sight of my arms and legs was very disturbing. When I was finally strong enough to walk, I went outside and found a broken piece of mirror on the ground. To see my face was the most horrible thing. It did not even look human anymore. I wanted to commit suicide, but my belief in God encouraged me to live. It seemed that if God allowed me to live, I should have the courage to continue, no matter how hard it was.

Until May, we lived in the basement of the hospital with three families. My hearing came back but I was still very weak and sick. We were told to leave, but had no money and no place to go, so we stayed. My brother returned from China and found us living there. There was no one else in my family alive. I lost over fifty people. We could not find their bodies – not even their ashes. Together we built a small little hut and once I was better, I cared for my mother till her death.

In 1951, I got a job as a scrubwoman in a tuberculosis ward. It was very hard to work with people who looked healthy while I was so deformed. I had tuberculosis myself but was too poor to go to the hospital. I also suffered severely with gall bladder problems and many other problems with my internal organs. I was very lucky in 1958 to have an operation on my face and hands.

For a long time I was very bitter and hateful about the bombing. A few years ago, I was fortunate to have an audience with the Pope with several other survivors. He encouraged us to speak out about our experience and to use it as a lesson that may teach others who follow us. Many of us here in Nagasaki have travelled to many countries speaking for peace. Now the survivors are getting old and weak, so it's up to the next generation to carry on the work of peacemaking.

Tsuyo Kataoka.

I *feel that my life is wrapped up in a miracle. Every day things happen that I would have said were impossible. Living with such abandon is the most fulfilling experience I've ever had — to have all day to speak of things of the heart, things that run so deep they make me cry for joy or sadness, to be with people who surrender their lives to the common cause, to talk and talk till words run dry, then to pray, write, ponder, and board the train for the next stop where it starts all over with a fresh perspective. There is loneliness, of course, and times when I wonder what I'm doing so far away. But for the most part, I feel at home wherever I go. In fact, when people ask when I am going home, my first thought is, I am home.*

— JOURNAL ENTRY

TAKAMORI: A CATHOLIC-BUDDHIST RETREAT

I had the great privilege of spending three days at Takamori, a Catholic-Buddhist monastery in the Japanese alps. It is a small retreat/farm which has been hand-built by Father Oshida, a Dominican priest who left the comforts of urban life behind to create an environment for simple living, communal sharing, physical labor and meditation. Takamori means "grass hut," which is the first thing Father Oshida built when he went up into the mountains twenty years ago.

I first heard of Father Oshida when I was in Tsu-shi, staying with the Sisters of St. Joseph of Carondelet. They told me the story of his visit with the Dalai Lama, the spiritual leader of the Mahayanist Buddhists of Tibet. During the hour that the two were together, not a word was spoken. At the end of the hour, Dalai Lama asked if Father Oshida would please return again one day and honor him with another meeting.

When I heard this, I felt a great longing to find this man and be in his presence. The next morning I mentioned to a priest that I was interested in finding Father Oshida and he looked at me like I was crazy. Who was I to think I could spend time with a man of such greatness? More determined than ever, I found someone who knew his whereabouts and managed to get the phone number for Takamori.

After a few attempts, I finally got through and was practically speechless when I heard Father Oshida's quiet voice on the other end of the line. I explained to him that I was making a peace pilgrimage around the world and that I would love to spend some time working and praying at Takamori. He was very gracious and said to come anytime, that he would be most delighted to meet with me and have me stay for a while. The next day I was on a train heading up the mountains, wondering what it would be like to experience the juxtaposition of Catholic and Buddhist traditions.

When I arrived, Father Oshida was out working in the field. He was in his late sixties, but every day he put in several hours of physical labor.

I was met by a young Catholic sister who was very gracious and only spoke Japanese. We bowed at each other for several minutes until another woman came out of the kitchen. With delightfully broken English, she welcomed me and showed me to my room, a small partitioned space with a single bed, a tiny closet and a desk. After sleeping in people's living rooms for a couple of weeks, this arrangement looked truly extravagant to me.

Within an hour, a bell rang and someone came to show me the way to the chapel, a small building about fifteen by fifteen feet. There were ten people who came together for Vespers and *zazen*, the practice of sitting in meditation. We sat in a circle around the altar, which was merely a cloth on the floor in the center of the room. There were a few candles, some songbooks, a chalice and a water bowl. Scattered around the room were pillows to sit on.

After Vespers and about forty minutes of silent meditation, the bell rang again and it was time for dinner. We ate mostly vegetarian meals, prepared very simply with ingredients often supplied by neighbors and friends. My first night, however, was a special occasion, as someone down the road had caught an eel and barbecued it as a delicacy. I had second thoughts about eating eel, but once I surrendered and took the first bite, I thought I'd never again taste anything so delicious.

After dinner, Father sat down with the guests and residents for their spiritual teaching. Since it was conducted in Japanese, I didn't know what was being said, but I was aware of a great respect and attention present in the room. It was very humbling to be in a room where everyone else was so engaged, feeling on the outside of a very important conversation. I knew, though, that I was lucky to be there and had a lot to learn about humility and acceptance.

I slept very soundly that night and woke at 6 A.M. to the clanging of the bell. By the time I made it to the chapel, all the others were sitting cross-legged on the floor. At that hour, it was still below freezing at minus four degrees centigrade. I grabbed a pillow and sat on the outside edge of the circle so no one would notice if I made a mistake. After ten minutes, my legs started throbbing. I knew I'd never reach enlightenment. All I could focus on was my pain. As I looked around the room, I was surprised that no one else was shuffling around trying to get comfortable. They all had their eyes shut, their hands opened with palms up, and a look of great calm on their faces. How could they be so happy? Didn't they know I could see their breath? I was icy cold, totally preoccupied and feeling more crippled by the minute. Buddhism has a lot to offer, I thought, but this torture has got to go.

After what seemed like hours, a welcome voice broke the silence with the first strains of Gregorian chant. What a blessed relief to hear Latin again! Finally, a language I could understand, sounds that were familiar.... I felt like I was eighteen, singing in the choir at St. Anthony's Church. My pain disappeared immediately and all my grumbling turned to praise and thanksgiving. We sang for twenty minutes, then said Lauds and began the Mass. Once it was all over, I was full of vitality and determined to get this zazen thing down pat.

During the day, we worked in the fields gathering straw and laying it out to dry in golden fan-shaped sections. Once the sun had done its part, we piled it into wheelbarrows and hauled it to the storage bins. I worked with two seminarians who didn't speak English, but we had a great time joking and talking in signs. I never thought I could feel so close to people I couldn't speak with, but I soon learned that speech is only one small part of communication. Praying, working and playing together need no common words.

That evening during Father Oshida's spiritual teaching, he asked if I had any questions. I told him that I was struggling with the question of Christianity versus Buddhism and that I often felt torn between the two, not knowing which path to choose. I wondered how he reconciled the Christian mandate to "go and teach all nations" with the Buddhist tradition of silence and meditation. Maybe I should be living a quieter life, creating peace through prayer and meditation instead of making this peace journey around

LEFT: Seminarian laying out the rice to dry.

BELOW: Father Oshida coming in from the fields.

the world. Maybe all my efforts to make a difference in the world were really futile and that what I should really do is try to make a difference in myself.

He explained that the point is not to convert the world but to convert our souls to God. He spoke of Christ as the *event* of Buddhist thought.

"Stop trying to interpret things so literally and put your attention on the event," he said. "Experience the event, experience your life and everything around you as an incarnation. Do not try to think this out with your mind. Let yourself go deeper so that you might experience wisdom. It is our work to reach new levels of depth and to go beyond what we have learned to be true. All religions are the same, though Christians have been responsible for most war and death."

I began to practice his advice during the meditations, attempting to experience my body in all its discomfort. I stopped focusing on how I wanted it to be different and started paying attention to how it was. Once I stopped resisting, the pain subsided. I could never understand how this worked, but when I remember his words, the message is clear: "Don't be concerned with understanding it — just be with what's happening."

By the time I left Takamori, I was no longer in a quandary about my trip. I knew I needed to act at this time, out of my belief that we *are* one another's keepers, that the quality of our relationships with one another *does* make a difference in the world and that big changes always start with small conversations. The time I had spent in meditation freed me from unnecessary concerns and I went on my way more fully alive to the present.

Schoolgirls row down the Motoyasu River in Hiroshima.

The American teachers over here often warn me that the Japanese are shy and witholding, reluctant to ask questions or engage in dialogue, so that I'm not disappointed when total silence follows my presentation. So far, my experience has always been a flood of response and a real sense of oneness with the people. I think it's the Americans who keep that from happening. If one feels different, then there is a difference. I haven't met anyone yet I didn't have something in common with. It just takes more time to uncover it with some people.

— JOURNAL ENTRY

THE GIRLS SCHOOL IN TSU-SHI

I spent a few days in Tsu-shi with the Sisters of St. Joseph of Carondelet who run a school for girls in grades seven through nine and a nursery school for children one through five years old. It was a very American convent, with all the comforts of home. I slept in my first bed in weeks, since I had been staying with Japanese families who sleep on little mattresses on the floor. The convent bathtub was also Western-style – another surprise, as I had gotten used to the Japanese model, a short, stubby square unit that you sit in *after* you've washed and rinsed off outside.

I spoke to the freshmen girls one morning and was amazed at their perfect behavior. The students start class by standing and saying "Please teach us." We watched the slideshow *Focus on Peace* and there was a Japanese woman there who had been at the 1982 Disarmament Rally in New York City. She lived nearby and when she heard I was showing the slideshow, she asked to come and interpret. The students were excited to see all the teenagers from the United States and Canada involved in peace work. "I did not know there was such a thing as a peace movement in America," said one girl. "Why do we not hear news like this from your country? We would think differently about Americans maybe."

Being outside of the United States gives one an opportunity to see how our country is perceived by other people. Though the Japanese, in general, have a tendency toward reticence, I spoke with many who had serious questions about American policies around the world. It was hard for them to understand the many different opinions that Americans hold on every issue. In Japanese culture, individuality is discouraged. Each profession, each school, each store has its uniform. Even in religion, people can't relate to one God or to the individuality of soul. Personal feelings are not valued highly, and what is good for the whole group is most important.

The students in Tsu-shi thought that I must agree with everything going on in my country. How puzzled they looked when I explained that I do not believe that war is necessary. How their brows furrowed when I spoke of the world being our production; that each of us, in a way, is responsible for how it looks and what is happening. We are inventing the world and our job is to collaborate in the event. We are only as powerless as we act, and if enough people were committed to ending war on this planet, it would end.

The girls were amazed to hear this kind of talk. They giggled, as they always did when they didn't know what else to do. They had learned all their lives to be demure and docile. Had anyone ever told them how powerful they were? How much potential they had to make change and create history?

My whole life was changed in the sixties when a teacher, Sister Robert Joseph, challenged my English composition class: "This is your *Life* – this is not a dress rehearsal. Get with it. *Use* your life. Live it with passion. Fall in love with the beauty of this earth." After her classes, I was never the same. And I was committed to making that kind of a difference in the lives of the students I stood before.

I could not tell what these girls understood or absorbed. I knew they were moved by the photographs and that something changed for them when they saw images of so many people standing for peace. They often cried, and, embarassed by their emotions, kept their thoughts to themselves. I often cried, too, and there would be long moments when we bowed our heads, unable to speak. It was a ritual, performed over and over, and yet never the same. The ones who spoke didn't say much, but their messages were powerful:

"I always felt alone until now. Somehow I don't feel so alone anymore."

"If grownups are so smart, why are we in such a mess?"

"I don't want to live in a world where I have to be afraid of bombs. Now I guess I must do something to get rid of them."

"I used to write poetry about love and things. Now I will try to write about what is going on in the world."

"I never thought about peace before because I thought war was the answer to problems between countries. Thinking of a world without war makes me happy and excited."

When the class was over, several girls stayed behind, wondering if I could stay longer and make a presentation to their parents. They didn't think they could explain it well enough without pictures. Unfortunately, I had a train to catch to Kyoto, so they were on their own. And I have a feeling that they told the story very well.

Young schoolgirl plays with a pinecone as she walks through one of Tokyo's many clean subway stations.

Japan has been a very special stop, a place to learn how different my own culture is, to appreciate the freedom that I take for granted, to question what oppression of women means to me and why. The struggle is in trying to accept and appreciate this culture and balance that with my feelings about the pervasive pornography and the status of women here.

Women have told me that they obey their father until they have a husband to obey. Though many women work in the companies, few hold executive jobs, and most are hired to make tea and perform secretarial tasks. Because it is a culture of non-confrontation, where it is of primary importance to accept things as they are, it doesn't occur to many women to challenge the system. I can't help but wonder if this is how they really want it to be or if they wouldn't prefer more respect and freedom. It's been hard not speaking Japanese and wanting to have these kinds of conversations with women.

I have many questions as I leave, but one thing I know for sure — our gestures toward equality in the United States look like Himalayan successes from here.

— JOURNAL ENTRY

Beijing Morning Bird. I met her at dawn in a city park. She was standing on the edge of a hill, wailing out a Chinese opera. When she saw me, she stopped and smiled, then went right on singing.

MAKING FRIENDS IN BEIJING

Before I left home, a doctor from Syracuse gave me the address of Dr. Zhang, a professor in Beijing who had three daughters studying at Syracuse University. I wrote to him from Japan and asked to meet him when I got to Beijing. He responded quickly, inviting me to stay in the apartment of a daughter who was out of the country. Six weeks later, when my train pulled into Beijing, he and two sons-in-law were standing there to greet me.

Our first stop was the police station, since I had to be registered in order to stay in a Chinese apartment. To have a foreigner mix with the Chinese was very extraordinary, but somehow he had managed to get permission from the authorities. From there we went to get a month's bus pass, and then on to his daughter's apartment, where another of his daughters had prepared a scrumptious six-course lunch on a two-burner hot plate.

Dr. Zhang has five daughters. All are named Wei and referred to as Daughter Number One, Daughter Number Two, Daughter Number Three, etc. I soon became Daughter Number Six. Wei's apartment was many miles from Dr. Zhang's and there were no phones, so we had to arrange our appointments very carefully. With a bicycle and bus pass to get around the city, I was rarely home.

We met about twice a week and spent the days walking through parks, visiting the few remaining palaces and temples. He said there weren't many left since the Cultural Revolution, when Mao Tse-tung's Red Guard tore through the country destroying everything from the past, including museums, temples, palaces and works of art.

Mao's plan was to create a classless, prosperous and idealistic society, where goods were produced and owned collectively and available to all as needed. Communism in China did, in fact, eliminate starvation, a problem that had plagued this country for centuries. But the damage that was done over the years of *The Great Leap Forward* is still a painful memory for many who lived through it.

Being objective about the state of affairs in China would not come naturally, I knew, given the anti-communist propaganda I'd been exposed to all my life. So I was determined to spend as much time with the people as I could to hear from them about their lives.

One difficulty was that the Chinese are strongly discouraged from spending time with foreigners. Dr. Zhang felt safe enough, since I had been cleared with the local authorities, but he said we should not talk about politics when we were walking down the street. Another friend of mine, Fook Che, always preferred to meet me in places away from his own neighborhood. He'd say, "I'll ride my bicycle in front of the Friendship Store at three o'clock and you follow me on yours." Then we'd ride for miles until he felt comfortable about being seen with me.

Fook Che was a classical pianist in a club that catered to American businesspeople and embassy personnel. The joint venture negotiators were always frustrated with the Chinese for spending so much time on rhetoric and not respecting their "time is money" approach to work. Being a pianist, Fook Che made four dollars a week for twelve hours work, the same amount I spent on an Irish Coffee when I went to hear him play. It was a part-time job he took to save money for a piano, though it would take years and years of saving. His full-time job was doing research for an encyclopedia on music composers around the world.

He lived with his family but couldn't take me to meet them since foreigners were not allowed in his home. We spent hours walking together, riding our bicycles, sitting in little restaurants lost in conversation, as he rhapsodized about his love for Bellow, Twain, Kafka, Tchaikovsky and Handel. Fook Che was gay, though he'd never been with a man, since homosexuality is forbidden in China. His country was like a prison to him, he said. He could not be himself, give his life to work he chose, go where he would like to go.

Being with me reminded him of his limitations, but also of his vitality and dreams. One night we were talking about how much we needed hugs. "Wouldn't it be great to start a Hug Company?" I said. "We could stand on the street corner and sell hugs for a dollar apiece." "Yeah! People would love it!" he cheered. "And if they're too shy, we can give them a pat on the back for a quarter." But then reality would set in and we'd be off, gone again into our own separate worlds. As melancholy as he got sometimes when he compared his life to mine, when he took his seat at the baby grand and played the first notes of the Moonlight Sonata, a look of great peace would wash over him and it seemed that all was perfect with Fook Che.

Dr. Y.L. Zhang from Beijing.

This culture is more challenging than anything I've been exposed to yet. It stirs up the ultimate questions about life and freedom, forcing me to unravel the roots of my thinking. Hundreds of mule-drawn carts carrying hay and a handful of peasants pass in front of these magnificent palaces, built for the emperors thousands of years ago. The Chinese are far behind technologically, doing most of the work by hand. It's common to see twenty to thirty men harnessed to a cart pulling massive pieces of equipment. Some people say the Cultural Revolution is to blame, since it brought education to a standstill for ten years, except for the study of Mao's Red Book.

It's hard to tell what the commonfolk feel, since I only talk with people who are educated enough to speak English, and the intellectuals suffered terribly during the revolution. I suppose if I talked with someone who was starving before the revolution and whose family now has enough to eat, they would not be critical of a change that saved their lives.

— JOURNAL ENTRY

THE CHRISTMAS JOURNEY

On Christmas day, I was on a thirty-six hour train ride from Shanghai to Guanyinzhou. For the first time in months, I felt both lonely and alone. I thought playing Christmas carols on my harmonica might help, but it only made things worse. I knew there had to be someone on the train who understood the meaning of Christmas and would like to celebrate, so I went on a search through twenty-one cars. I looked every passenger in the eye, hoping to find a kindred spirit, but no luck.

My head ached from listening to high-pitched Chinese music blaring through rattling speakers, I was sick with a terrible cold, and there was no one on the whole train I could talk to. I went back to my bunk for a nap, hoping something more fun would happen in my dreams. Right before I went to sleep, I heard "You Are My Sunshine," my family's favorite singalong, through the scratchy old speakers. I felt then, for the first time, a lightness that felt like someone was out there wishing me well.

I slept soundly till the train stopped and hordes of people got on and off. Once we were on our way again, I sat up to have some tea, which porters cart around in huge containers. As I looked down the aisle, I could hardly believe my eyes when I saw the back of a blonde head. Leaping from my bunk, I flew down the aisle to check it out. What a thrill to find an Englishman! He was a student of Chinese and quite fluent, so we sat up half the night telling stories, singing Christmas carols and talking with our neighbors.

Finding him was like a miracle. I had longed for the opportunity to sit and talk with ordinary Chinese people, to ask them questions about their lives and get a deeper understanding of their interesting culture. And now here was the chance. Ted, the Englishman, was thrilled to be my interpreter, and several folks crowded around taking part in the festivities as we toasted the holiday and shared our lives. After a few hours, I returned to my bunk, crawled into my sleeping bag and fell sound asleep, exhausted , as my mother used to say, "from having so much fun."

In the bunk across from me was a ninety-year-old woman and her sixty-five-year-old son who were on their way to Hong Kong to visit her other son. When they boarded the train, the son carried her in and placed her on the bunk across from me. As he gently removed her tiny slippers, the sight of her once-bound, disfigured feet made me cry. I turned away so she wouldn't notice and lay there quietly weeping at the thought of all that pain.

Her son was tender with her, always attentive, always asking if she wanted tea or crackers. We became very close early on, even though I couldn't talk with them. I sang them songs and played tunes on my harmonica, which they loved and always applauded. She slept most of the time, but whenever she was awake, she let me sit by her side and hold her hand. I read words out of my Chinese dictionary, trying to piece together sentences I thought she'd understand. I don't think she ever knew what I was saying, but she was happy that I was there saying *something*.

The Chinese are great gift-givers, and these two were loaded with presents for their Hong Kong relatives. They stashed most of them under their bed, including two shoeboxes, which were tied with string and punctured with holes. The first evening they came on board, a strange swishy flopping noise woke me up in the middle of the night. At first, I thought I was dreaming, but eventually the noise got louder and louder. Terrorized by my imagination, I couldn't imagine anything nice that made that kind of sound. Reaching down to the bottom of my sleeping bag, I grabbed my little yellow flashlight and shone the light on the floor beside me. Six inches from my head was a twenty-inch long fish trying to jump up on my bunk. I screamed, waking up everyone around and before long ten people in their nightclothes were scrambling around trying to capture the fish. The next morning, the two shoeboxes were gone and the son had left a little bag of candies next to my pillow.

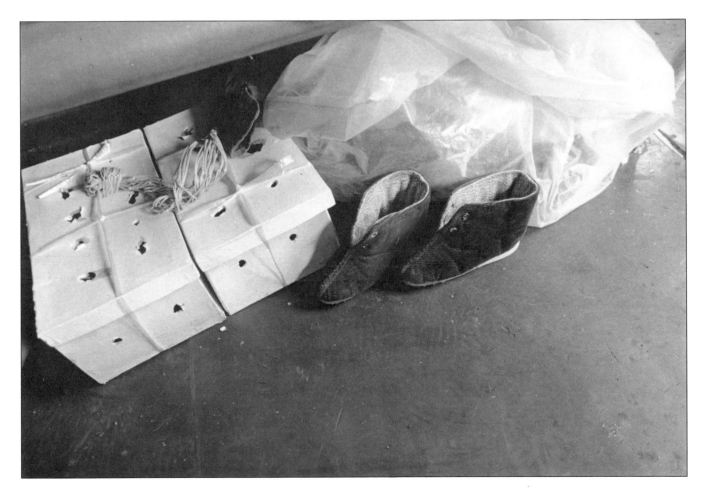

View from my bunk of my neighbor's fish boxes and his
mother's tiny shoes for her once-bound feet.

I'd often go to the park at dawn to watch the elders welcome the day. They'd start arriving before it was light, shadowless figures in the gray mist. I'd hear nothing but the shuffle of shoes and the canes of women whose feet had once been bound. They gathered in groups, and without a word, someone would start. Their bodies, in unison, would begin the meditative movement of tai chi.

Shanghai Park, China.

Every morning at 10 A.M., revolutionary music is broadcast over the city's public address systems. Children all leave their classrooms and run around several blocks. I never knew if this routine was to wake them up or calm them down. I was told that all residents were encouraged to stop what they were doing and exercise during this time, but I never saw many people cooperating with the exercise program in Beijing.

— JOURNAL ENTRY

Wei's apartment.

I went to dinner at Wei's house tonight. She and her husband are both artists. Together they prepared an eight-course meal, almost outdoing her mother, who's the best cook I've ever met. Neither Wei nor her husband speak any English, but since food and art are so universal, it didn't matter that we couldn't talk to each other.

I brought my slides over to share and we didn't have a projector, so they held them up to the light and looked at every one, chatting to each other the whole time. It was also fun to share the photographs of my family. No matter what the language, people always understand mother, father, sister and brother.

The hall lights go off at ten o'clock in this apartment house, and there are no elevators, so I have to carry my bicycle up eight flights of stairs in the dark when I'm late, which I do nearly every night. The Chinese don't stay out late, but I found an International Club where foreigners get together, so I have a chance to speak English.

Tonight after I was home for a while, I heard a knock at the door. It was the police again. This is their third time this week. It's always the same. I open the door and they talk Chinese to me. I say, "I don't understand a word you're saying," and they don't know what I'm talking about. Then I get my passport and registration. They stare at it for a few mintues, then look around the apartment to make sure I'm not entertaining anybody. "I should be so lucky," I always say and they walk out, just as serious as they walked in.

Now I know what Robert Louis Stevenson meant when he said: "I travel not to get places, but to climb down off the featherbed of civilization."

— JOURNAL ENTRY

China is so complex, with so many distinctions between the past and the present. The Great Wall, the ancient temples and tombs, the palaces filled with the most precious gems, costumes, art ... people herd by the thousands to these sights, gazing with awe at their history, pausing to have a photo taken while sitting in a car pretending for a moment that such a luxury would be accessible. Communism has not changed the fantasies.

Nor has it put an end to sexism in this country. The women work side by side with the men, carrying hundred-pound bags of rice, driving trucks, building bridges. Liberated for work but not for leisure, their work day continues into the night as they prepare meals, do the dishes, wash the laundry. So much for the Cultural Revolution.

— Journal entry

Bicyclists in Tiananmen Square, Beijing.

I notice that people here are very distrustful of each other. The state has such power in their lives, more control than I could ever stand to live with, given who I am today. Some families that I've visited have been so cautious, afraid their neighbors may turn them in for entertaining a foreigner.

On Christmas Eve I was sharing dinner with a family in Shanghai. The daughter, who is thirteen years old, asked if she might go to church for Midnight Mass. I was surprised to hear there was a Mass going on and offered to take her with me. The father said no. He thought it would not be safe. People might see and then there'd be trouble. I was sad and angry, but powerless to change the situation. My first impulse was to say: "Forget what your neighbors might do. Forget about the repercussions that might come from the authorities. Follow your heart. Go to pray and be with people to celebrate your faith. This is a time for joy and communion, not fear and secrecy."

I never said those things because I know how serious it is to fall out of grace with the authorities. Little freedoms reward proper behavior in China and great limitations follow inappropriate behavior. Perhaps how it occurred to the father was that his good behavior resulted in a good position at the Music Institute and a chance for his daughter to choose her career instead of being directed by the state, as is common for so many.

Perhaps for him, the choice was for a lifetime rather than an evening. Perhaps it is that serious and I have no right to judge, standing on the outside with little at stake.

When I was in the novitiate, I used to complain about our lack of freedom. "Why must we meditate at such an hour? Why must we be silent after night prayers? Why can we only drink Pepsi when visitors are here? I would be much happier with more freedom, then I would make a better sister." My novice director would reply, "The wise person is one who is chained to a tree and finds her freedom even in that."

I understand that better after being in China.

– JOURNAL ENTRY

Sunset at Ko Samui

PARADISE FOUND

When I returned to Hong Kong, my American friend Diana joined me and we flew to Thailand for a month in the sun. After five weeks of China's Siberian winds and sub-zero temperatures, I was ready for Ko Samui, a magical little island in the Gulf of Siam. It took a day and a half from Bangkok, by train, bus and ferry.

There were armed guards to ward off train robbers and I felt like I was in a Jesse James movie. Paranoid about our cameras being stolen, we both went to bed with all our gear in the bottom of our sleeping bags. The bunks seemed comfortable in the station, but once the train started rocking down the track, it was like trying to sleep in a Tilt-A-Whirl.

What a relief, I thought, to get off the train and onto a bus. Little did I know. The bus seats were so close together, my knees were pressed tight against the seat in front. And the roads were so bumpy that the bus was off the ground half the time. The luggage kept falling off the racks and crashing down on people who were wrapped around each other like pretzels because about seventy of us were crammed into a fifty-passenger vehicle. Thank God the bus ride lasted only two hours.

The next ride was on a ferry more overcrowded than the bus. It listed so badly that people were clinging to anything to keep from falling down. After nineteen hours, we arrived on Ko Samui, sweaty, grimy and ready for a swim.

Every lodge on the island had people meeting the ferry, announcing their indisputable deals to prospective customers. We jumped into the pickup heading for Lipa Lodge as soon as we heard they had bungalows for four dollars a night. Ours was a beautiful bamboo hut, nestled in the palms about twenty feet from the water. It had two double beds, electricity, running water, a shower and fan. There was an open cabana on the beach for dining and the food was fresh caught, fresh picked and absolutely delicious.

Our first meal was fresh crab, shrimp fried rice, fried squid and sumtom, an exquisite salad made from shredded young papaya, crushed peanuts, red chilis, coriander, lime juice and fermented fish sauce. The total bill was less than the price of three Big Macs. That night we decided to stay at Lipa until we'd tried everything on the menu.

The next day we meandered along the beach, collecting shells and watching the fishermen mend their nets. The island was like one big coconut grove in the middle of the Gulf and a community of saffron-robed Buddhist monks lived next to us in the palm forest.

ADVENTURE IN KO PHANGAN

One day we decided to visit a neighboring island, Ko Phangan, three hours away by ferry. It's smaller and more primitive than Ko Samui, with no cars, no electricity, and no business but fish and coconuts.

Someone had told us to look for Mr. Poo, a short, bald man with black gums and no teeth (effects of too much betelnut) who had rooms on the beach. He was standing on the shore as our boat pulled in, so we walked up and asked if he had a double. He nodded and led us down the beach to his row of bamboo huts. We gave him twenty baht (about one dollar), left our gear, rented an old wooden rowboat and went off on a snorkeling spree.

Later that evening we ran into a man from California who told us about a beautiful beach on the eastern side of the island. The next morning we began our trek to Seaview, Panghan East.

Walking down the main street of town with clothespins holding up our sarongs and cameras swinging from our necks and shoulders, we were quite the sight to the local folk. Someone with a Honda 90 offered to give us a lift and the three of us rode through coconut groves for a few miles, squished together like sardines. He dropped us off at an isthmus where the path stopped and headed back. There we were, stranded, and not a clue about where to go.

Suddenly an old man about eighty, toothless and barefoot, shouted something at us and pointed ahead with his scythe-like bamboo cutter. This meant to follow him. We walked for two hours, often up to our waists in the gulf, holding all our gear and cameras above our head. Finally the old man pointed into the jungle and motioned for us to keep walking. There was only one path so we followed it, right by a pit of water buffalo and several huts with menageries of pigs, dogs and roosters, all excited about our arrival.

The path ended up in someone's yard and I yelled up to the woman on the porch, "Where's the Seaview?" By this time, all the dogs in the area were barking at us and whatever she shouted back, I didn't understand. The pigs were on their way over for a visit, so we left abruptly, deciding to find it on our own. Another mile or so and we reached Seaview, a little hideaway on a gorgeous bay. We cleaned up, drank a warm beer, had some roast squid and noodles, then fell into bed as the sun touched the sea. The end of a perfect day in Ko Phangan.

Our journey back was easier since we knew the trail, and we made it back to Mr. Poo's in time for dinner. We photographed him and his family and he was so grateful he wouldn't take our money for the cabin. In the morning he woke us at 4:00 A.M. so we could catch the ferry to Ko Samui.

In a few hours we were back, ordering breakfast at the Darin Restaurant. The special was toast with garlic and jam. What a way to start the day....

"I went to Bangkok for law school when I was young and thought I liked the noise; now I'm old and now I know this is where I want to be, by the sea where it's quiet." Siri Pan Tanawanishanam, Mr. Poo's daughter, is twenty-eight years old.

It's hard to imagine there's another world out there, where there are things to do beyond exploring beaches, watching monkeys pick coconuts, trying to decide on fresh crab or roast squid. I realize how out of touch I am with the world, not having read a newspaper for two weeks or talked to anyone who has a sense of the larger picture. All I can do is trust it's going well out there. It's getting easier to let it go, to relax into the zen of the changing tides. I'm happy, peaceful and everything I know is enough for now.

— JOURNAL ENTRY

NORTH TO CHIANG MAI

After our holiday in paradise, we decided to head north for a trek into the mountains where the hill tribes live. We took a bus from Bangkok to Chiang Mai and within hours I was sick with food poisoning from sausage I ate in a German-Thai restaurant. For two days I thought I was going to die and wished I would.

A friend in Hong Kong had given me the name of a woman who was teaching at the university in Chiang Mai and when I called her, she invited us over for some ginger rice soup and cookies. Once I was able to get out of bed, we walked over to her house and spent a few hours learning about life in Thailand from one who had lived there many years.

The people have absolute loyalty to their king and act with great deference to authority in general. The first time this woman attended a graduation at the college, the king was going to make a brief presentation. Now when the king is around, people not only bow, but they lie face down on the floor to show their respect. That evening, the stage was so full of bodies lying all over the floor that the man with the microphone had a difficult time stepping over all of them. Later, at a party where other honorable guests were present, the students serving drinks spent the whole evening hobbling around the living room on their knees.

We found it comical, but I'm sure we have customs in the U.S. that must seem ridiculous to outsiders. What must they think of our Halloween antics, or the sight of Catholics genuflecting and kissing their bishop's ring, or our boxing events where huge crowds of people cheer while two men beat each other senseless?

Traditions become significant and sacred rituals in each country. In the act of ritualizing, we forego our egos and selfish concerns, acting as one, for the good of the whole. Simultaneous participation in a single event re-creates a sense of the solidarity that bonds us as members of the human family. It allows us to be fully alive – not a body alone, but a spirit in harmony with the rest of the world.

Religion is a dominant force in Thailand, symbolized by the ever present wat, or Buddhist temple. Saffron-robed Buddhist monks are a common sight, as every male is supposed to spend some time in temple service, and there are hundreds of thousands of monks and novices throughout the country. At certain times of day you see them walking the streets with their copper begging bowls, dependent on others' generosity for their daily sustenance.

Espousing a religion of enlightenment, Buddhists do not believe, but understand; they do not worship, but practice what they understand. One of the principles of Buddhism is to seek enlightenment so that all humanity is benefited and all sentient beings mercifully treated. Ignorance is seen as the root of suffering and meditation as the means to eliminating ignorance. A natural consequence of this understanding is an emphasis on serene, humble and virtuous behavior. The monks are full of spirit and a joy to encounter, exuding a radiant peacefulness wherever they go.

Animism, a religion based on belief in spirits, predates Buddhism but still permeates Thailand's culture. Beautifully adorned spirit houses are everywhere, containing an assortment of foods and trinkets to please the spirits. Brahmanism, imported from India, is another religion that has provided many popular ceremonies as well as a variety of heavens and hells within the grasp of everyone. So there is no shortage of religions, and the Thais do not distinguish among the various components. To them, it is all part of a whole, and it suffices to feel, believe and enjoy.

To be in a country where people really *celebrate* their faith, where festivals and rituals are sources of great joy and comfort, where people combine elements of many religions to bear common witness to the sacredness of life — that, to me, was being in a holy land.

Karen tribeswoman
winnowing rice.

A TREK TO THE HILL TRIBES

We found a Burmese guide who took us into the mountains to visit the hill tribe people. After nine years of fighting, he left the Burmese Revolutionary Army and married a woman from the Yellow Lahu tribe. He called himself David and wore yellow rubber flip-flops.

On the day of departure, we met at a restaurant for coffee, then caught a bus to Chiang Dao, a few hours north. From there, we hopped a mini-bus and rode to the end of the line. At that point, we waited for our next connection, a Toyota pickup, which arrived in a cloud of dust an hour later, already loaded with twenty-two passengers. We squeezed in and bounced along in good natured unison for another ten miles. Once we jumped off the dusty truck, the trek on foot began and soon we were up to our waists fording a stream.

The first village we came to was the home of the Shan tribe. They left Burma in 1980 after fighting with the government for independence. There were fifty-seven families in the village we visited, creating a community of about three hundred people. Most of them are involved in agriculture, growing rice, soya and sesame, but many engage in smuggling and drug trafficking, which is more profitable and convenient since the Thai-Burmese border is only a few miles away.

Further up the road, we came to the White Karen tribe, which originated in Tibet over two centuries years ago. They migrated to Burma and then Thailand, where they now grow rice in the mountains. The Karens work the land for three years, then move to another spot for richer soil. They have no machinery, so they do all their work by hand, though there are only nine families left.

After a short break at the Karen village, we were off again to climb what David referred to as "baby mountains." To me they were uninviting vertical inclines and I wished he had warned us in advance about the difficulty of the climb. I probably wouldn't have started out if I knew how hard it was going to be.

From far up front, David looked back at the two of us, bedraggled and discouraged, and shouted, "Just ten more minutes."

"I guess we can make it," I said to Diana, my body drenched in sweat, my good humor long gone. Red-faced and panting, bent over like a hunchback with the weight of her pack, her sneakers squeaking with every step, she looked at me. "Ten minutes? Yeah, I guess we can make it."

Miles later, I checked my watch and an hour had passed. "David," I shouted up, "it's been an *hour*." "Ten more minutes," he called back, skipping along in his flip-flops. Later, I shouted up again, "David, how much longer?" "Ten more mintes," he responded. After another hour had passed, I screamed out in a rage, "David, stop!! It's getting dark. You keep saying ten more minutes, but we've gone for two hours and we're still not there. Why do you get our hopes up by lying to us?

He was slightly amused by my outburst. "I tell you ten more minutes because then you think you can do it. If I say three more hours you think you should turn back. You think you are not strong enough. This is not a lie. This is the only way I know to keep you going."

I was so exhausted and angry, nothing would have satisfied me at that point. "Well, we're not going to turn back now. We could never make it before dark. So tell me the truth this time – how much longer till we get to where we're going?" He smiled and started back up the hill. "Ten more minutes," he calmly replied.

We arrived at the village of the Yellow Lahus long after the sun had set over the Thailand-Burma border, which by this time we were very near. The people had built a fire and were preparing for a ritual dance to celebrate the last night of the new year. As with the other tribes, their survival depends on the goodness of the seasons and the kindness of the earth, so they celebrate rituals to dramatize their kinship with the earth and their great gratitude for a kind season.

An interesting twist is that five years earlier, when the tribe was still in Burma, their

Preparing food after Sunday morning Mass.

rice crop failed and they suffered a great famine. A Catholic missionary group arrived to bring them food and medicine, and the people converted to Catholicism to show their appreciation. So the Yellow Lahus, along with celebrating pagan holidays with opium and dancing around an open fire, celebrate Catholic Mass every Sunday in their bamboo chapel.

It was Saturday night when we arrived and David showed us to our room, the second story of a bamboo barn that housed four water buffalo, three pigs and a host of chickens and roosters, which I could see through the cracks in the floor. The buffalo were tied to the posts that held it altogether, so when they moved, we moved. The pigs and water buffalo snorted all night and the roosters started crowing before sunrise, so we didn't get much sleep.

At 7:30 the bell rang, waking people up for Mass. Diana and I dragged ourselves to the chapel, surprised to see the women and children on one side and the men on the other. There were fourteen plaques around the walls for the Stations of the Cross and in front was a huge map of Thailand, a sixteen-by-twenty-inch full-color photograph of the king and a picture

of Jesus. There are no priests, so the village appointed someone as religion master, who read dutifully out of a book for thirty minutes while men talked to each other, children crawled around and women spit through the cracks in the floor. Everything was done in the tribal language so I had no idea what was going on. After the reading they sang a few songs, but there wasn't much of a feeling of celebration. Nothing like the night before around the fire.

Two children from the Shan tribe.

My mother's birthday was coming up and I decided to write a song in her honor. I walked to town one day and bought a small guitar for fifteen dollars. It only stayed in tune for about ten minutes, but was better than nothing. I spent an afternoon working on her song, then I taped it, wrapped up the cassette and walked back to the Post Office in town to mail it. This is the song:

When I'm walking down the road somedays and see the setting sun
there's a question in my mind sometimes about what I've left undone
I wonder if I've made it clear to those I've left behind
just how very much I feel you here and hold you in my mind.

And I want to say thank you for your kindness, thank you for your dreams
the love that you are sending rushes through me like a stream
it flows into my morning hours and takes me through the day
at night it's like a candle, lighting up my way.

I'm heading for the mountaintop, moving toward the light
and the truth that I was seeking is moving into sight
I know I had it with me long before I started out
but I'm learning from the bottom up what faith is all about.

And I want to say thank you for believing, thank you for your love
I'm soaring on the breezes, flying like a dove
if it weren't for all you've given me, the strength you've handed down
I never would have found the wings to get me off the ground.

And though I'm often by myself, I never feel alone
your spirit's here beside me and I feel like I'm at home
when I hear a song we used to sing, I know you're doing well
and it feels just like a miracle, near as I can tell.

And I want to say thank you for your goodness, thank you for your care
there's some who call it energy, some who call it prayer
but there's something to this spirit that's holy as it's free
and this journey that I'm making is for you as well as me.

The streets of Manila are full of children hawking cigarettes and candy, unable to attend school because their families need the income. These schoolgirls, giving the sign for liberation from such poverty and injustice, are among the lucky ones to be well-fed and educated.

CHANGING TIMES IN THE PHILIPPINES

I hadn't planned to go to the Philippines, but during my visit to Hong Kong in January, I met a Catholic nun who convinced me my journey wouldn't be complete without a trip to her country. She made arrangements for me to stay with her community, an order of Franciscans who administered a college, high school, kindergarten and novitiate in Quezon City. By February 1, I was on my way to Manila.

For two weeks I lived in the novitiate, taking part in an "exposure program" set up by the sisters to provide me with some background on the political ferment that was occurring. At this time, massive opposition to President Ferdinand Marcos was developing and huge groups of people were protesting the presidential monopoly of power, the subservience of their government to foreign interests and the increasing incidents of military atrocities.

Peasants from the countryside were arriving by the busload to demonstrate with schoolteachers, business professionals, fishermen, clergy, students, the unemployed and the urban poor, each responding to the crisis of their own particular situation. Overnight vigils and rallies were common, with tens of thousands of people assembling to show their unity and demand changes. During the two weeks I was there, I spent time with many persons who were among the multitudes seeking an end to injustice.

One day I visited Manila's city dump, a slow burning mountain of fly-infested garbage, in Balut, Tondo. The people call it Smokey Mountain because the methane that's produced as the garbage decomposes causes it to burn continuously. Over 6,300 people live there, trying to eke out a living from the scraps of recyclable materials. The children can't go to school because they're needed to work all day. They spend their days separating the paper from the cans, washing the plastic in the stagnant waters nearby, and pulling carts full of tin from one site to another. This is their life and future.

Smokey Mountain.

Residents of Smokey Mountain, Manila's garbage dump, where over six thousand people live on what they can scavenge from recyclable scraps. The children are needed for work, so most cannot attend school. An eight-hour day on the foul, rat-infested heap earns them about twenty pesos, less than two dollars.

I spent two days reading old newspapers, trying to get a handle on the history of things since August, when the people's movement took on a new energy in the wake of ex-Senator Benigno Aquino's assassination. Though the escalating economic crises have certainly given momentum to the opposition, it's the image of Aquino's broken body lying on the tarmac that seems to be giving it heart. Without the benefit of a charismatic leader or clearly defined organizational structure, the people united have managed to cast an ominous shadow on the president's public image.

It's interesting to be an American here, photographing banners that read OUST THE U.S. BACKED MARCOS REGIME. Sometimes I feel suspended between two worlds.

— JOURNAL ENTRY

One of the issues facing farmers is loss of land they have tilled for generations. The lands they have cleared and made productive have been taken over and set up as export crop plantations owned by corporations, many of them American.

Unable to compete with the multinational agribusiness firms spreading like wildfire throughout their country, the peasants had no choice but to migrate to overcrowded urban areas. Soon, they were living in cardboard huts around the city perimeters, becoming part of a vast, exploited labor force if they were lucky, joining the ranks of the unemployed if not. As the people were being drawn into a maelstrom of poverty and homelessness, their leader was getting rich from making deals with foreign investors. And an anti-government, anti-American attitude was being generated among the people.

One day I visited Angel Carlos, the Secretary of PANAMA, the Union of the People of Navotas. Thirty-five thousand families in his area were about to be displaced by a road being built to service a Japanese-owned fishing port. The port was being remodeled into a totally mechanized facility, threatening the jobs of two thousand Filipinos.

"This is progress?" he asked. "This is right, to have other countries profit from our ports when our own people go hungry? Today it is easier to find a man searching through the garbage trying to stay alive than a dog. People are dying going without medicine, children being denied the right of going to school, living in huts made of cardboard. Isn't this violence against our people?"

Angel B. Carlos, general secretary of PANAMA, Union of the People of Navotas.

TOP LEFT: Aniano Javier, supervisor, Central Textile Mills, Inc. Employed by this company for 24 years, he's worked as a supervisor for 22 years. He still makes minimum wage, 39 pesos a day (about $2.73) The cost of living for a family of five is $4. per day. "If I were president, I'd make the military go away."

TOP RIGHT: Dante Quijano, mechanic, Central Textile Mills, Inc. Employed 25 years, still making the minimum wage, 39 pesos a day. "The only true thing in our newspapers anymore is the date."

LEFT: Sister Mariani Dimaranan, CFIC, founder and administrator of Task Force Detainees of the Philippines, a program providing services and support to political prisoners and their families. Sr. Mariani was arrested for subversion for speaking out about human rights in a college lecture. She was imprisoned for forty-seven days.

A*s the opposition leaders tack cautiously through the rough waters, deliberating over the leadership of a country on the edge of change, the winds of anger and disenchantment propel the people through the streets. The coalitions responsible for the hundreds of mass actions since Aquino's death have been rigorous in their campaign to educate as well as agitate for change. The people are beginning to understand the political and economic roots of the problems they wake up to daily.*

A country that has been viewed for generations as a land of naive peasants, a source of unchallenging cheap labor, is emerging into a nation of astute analysts, militant farmers, a labor force of politically conscious and capable workers grooming themselves for the next act in their revolutionary drama. They are moving slowly and deliberately, with grace, style and song, toward a final release from violence.

— JOURNAL ENTRY

The Roman Catholic Church has heightened her involvement as her leaders and laypeople respond to the accelerating crisis. No longer able to separate the political from the personal, the social from the sacred, the Church is engaging in a new form of intimacy with her people. Though a strain of traditionalism still exists, a movement toward change is coming from the roots and crown of this wakening monolith.

Christian base communities are emerging among the poor and working class, fostering the integration of spiritual and political awareness, the first step in transforming biblical covenants into social realities. I visited a center where a base community was meeting, where people were discussing the gospel promise in the light of their own social reality and under their own leadership.

One of the members explained to me afterward the unique value of these communities in the neighborhoods. She said that the Church was slow to respond to the crisis of the people, advocating patience and perseverance over upheaval and change. "But we are at the end of our rope. We are hungry, without jobs or food for our families. Many of us live in cardboard huts. It is our faith that tells us we deserve justice, we deserve dignity. Coming together to talk about our lives we can see that everything around us is violent. We have so little — not even human rights any more. And what good comes from Marcos's palace? He cares only for himself and the rich. The poor must live in violence every day. And when we come together to pray and share, it is for a way *out* of this violence that we pray. In faith, we must make a protest against this suffering."

The Sunday before I left the Philippines was Recollection Sunday for the Franciscans, and they had invited Father Louis Hechanova to lead a retreat. He mentioned the Church's changing role in achieving a national reconciliation based on justice, and acknowledged that, prior to Benito Aquino's assassination, the Church leaders were discussing reconciliation from a theological and pastoral perspective. Since then, he said, their attention had shifted to its political and social implications.

Referring to Jesus' directive to reconcile first with our sisters and brothers before we leave our gift at the altar, Father Hechanova said:

> *Sin is not something that divides us and God, but something that divides us among ourselves — and only because it divides us, it displeases God and becomes a sin against God as well. Today our concept of sin has expanded. It has to do with brokeness in our society. That situation does not yet reflect the full plan of God is a sinful situation, and we are expected to work not only for interpersonal, but also for structural reconciliation, so that the basis for what divides the Filipinos today — the clash of interests, the injustices, the corruption and exploitation, the tortures and killings — will be uprooted.*

Determining for themselves the political and economic future of their country will not be easy. Father Hechanova read a statement from a recently declassified U.S. document that made this task seem formidable. Though it was written four decades ago, he thought it represented a contemporary American attitude that Filipinos must understand if they are to negotiate with the United States about their future. The passage presents the general views of George Kennan on containment in Asia:

> We have about 50 percent of the world's wealth but only 6.3 percent of its population. This disparity is particularly great as between ourselves and the people of Asia. In this situation, we cannot fail to be the object of envy and resentment. Our real task in the coming period is to devise a pattern of relationship which will permit us to maintain this position of disparity, without positive detriment to our national security. To do so we will have to dispense with all sentimentality and daydreaming; and our attention will have to be concentrated everywhere on our immediate national objectives. We need not deceive ourselves that we can afford the luxury of altruism and world benefaction ... we should cease to talk about vague and unreal objectives such as human rights, the raising of living standards, and democratization. The day is not far off when we are going to have to deal in straight power concepts. The less we are then hampered by ideological slogans, the better.
>
> We should recognize that our influence in the Far Eastern area in the coming period is going to be primarily military and economic. We should make a careful study to see what parts of the Pacific and Far Eastern world are absolutely vital to our security, and we should concentrate our policy on seeing to it that those areas remain in hands we can control or rely on. ("Review of Current Trends. U.S. Foreign Policy, 2/24/48." Source: *Foreign Relations of the US, 1948*, I [part 2],523-26.)

The Filipinos' naivete about America's concern for them has been stripped away with their land, their cultural identity, their belief in a government loyal to their needs. They've lived with suffering for a long time. Now they are beginning to understand why, as they explore the complexities of their broken society.

After years of questionable leadership and foreign intervention, the flesh of a once rich country is nearly bone. Though poverty lingers at their nation's door, the people remain rich in spirit and hope, determined to reclaim their dignity and democracy. A bold and ascendant force, they are rising like a full moon, signalling the end of a dark era, the beginning of a new phase. The world is watching and there is much at stake, much to be learned from a people whose back is no longer bowed.

Tomorrow I leave Manila, a much different person than the one who arrived here two weeks ago. It's been wonderful living in community again, rising early for morning lauds, adoring the music the sisters make, loving the time I have to sit quietly in chapel, knowing I won't be disturbed.

It doesn't take long to get intimate, to reach the point where it's hard to say goodbye. I'm never not amazed at that kind of immediate warmth and kinship. Last night the sisters taped some new songs I'd written and this morning I was awakened by the sound of my own voice coming through the speakers. They are so dear and have touched my life very deeply, in so many ways.

When I first arrived in the Philippines, I considered myself a pacifist. I believed that people needed to be wildly imaginative in their response to oppression and that we of faith were called upon to gain freedom without the use of military force. Either way, I knew, many people died, as they did in India with Gandhi, trying to achieve justice through nonviolence. Everything I had ever learned told me killing was wrong, though I was never in a situation where my life was at stake. I understood that I came from a place of freedom and privilege, but I was very firm in my position and it would take a profound experience to change my my mind.

I understand now that those of us who live in comfort cannot preach patient endurance of a suffering that we ourselves are not asked to bear. I cannot judge for another when it is time to rise up or when to turn the other cheek. I cannot know the violence of poverty and injustice unless I myself am oppressed by it.

Sitting with these people, listening to their stories, seeing the hardship they bear, I am aware of the immense privilege guaranteed me as a white American. Where I take much for granted, the only thing these people know is that the quality of their lives and the lives of their children will never change unless they themselves are the agents of such change. The courage that the Filipinos are bringing to this task has been remarkable to witness and I will never be the same for having been here. To Sister Ludy, I am forever grateful for the part she played in getting me to her beautiful country.

Pilipinas, hindi ka nag-iis ... *Filipinas, you are not alone.*

— JOURNAL ENTRY

He was off to gather wood, a task that takes many hours and many
miles since there is such a scarcity of it in the mountains. Before he left,
we spent an hour in his garden eating fresh peas, drawing pictures and
learning to count in each other's language.

THE LAST HURRAH IN HONG KONG

I returned to Hong Kong from the Philippines, gathered all my belongings and said final goodbyes to the gracious Maryknoll sisters who had provided a wonderful refuge as I travelled to and from Hong Kong visiting other countries. I was leaving for Kathmandu at 7:00 A.M. and at six o'clock was bouncing along in a yellow cab, trying to drink coffee out of a styrofoam cup. Lugging my baggage from the curb to the counter was an ordeal in itself. I didn't realize until that chilly morning just how much I'd collected in China and Thailand.

When the man at the counter weighed my gear, it was forty pounds over the limit. "That'll be a hundred dollars for the extra baggage," he casually remarked. "A hundred dollars?!" I shrieked. "For forty pounds? You've got to be kidding! I don't have that kind of money to spare." "One hundred dollars," he repeated, "or leave your bags in Hong Kong."

I took off in search of a higher authority, knowing this was a mistake or a bribe. At that hour, however, there were no authorities to be found, time was runnning out and I had to find another solution. I headed back to the weighing station and picked up my bags, which now included a small guitar from Bangkok and a huge red, white and blue striped polyethylene bag from China, along with my king-size backpack and overstuffed camera bag.

I dragged them all into the ladies' restroom and started unloading everything that was small and heavy. I tore through my backpack, grabbing my fishing vest with thirteen pockets and a pair of army pants with pockets up and down each leg. I found another jacket that had six more pockets and, racing against time, I put them all on and started to load.

Camera lenses, cameras, tape recorders, cassette tapes, books, film and more film. I even stuffed a hiking boot with shampoo and paperbacks and loaded it in the pocket of my blue Goretex raincoat. Once I had every pocket filled, I shuffled out the restroom door, ruby-faced and drenched with sweat.

Dragging my guitar and backpack, I made my way to the scales, where the check-in man did a second take, a bit bewildered at my new appearance. He shook his head, weighed my baggage, and sure enough, it was two pounds under. With three minutes left to board, I thanked him, gathered my things and tried to hurry out the door. What a surprise when I got on the plane and couldn't fit into the tiny seats.

The man beside me tried to look casual, but his mouth hung open as he watched me unload. Out came the lenses, tape decks, cameras, cassette tapes, polaroid film packs, shampoo, books and one big hiking boot. I sat there quietly with it all on my lap, afraid to move till the plane took off. Once Hong Kong was a tiny city far below, I started repacking my heap of possessions. A half hour later, my pockets were empty. I took a deep breath and went right to sleep, happy to trade the horrors of the morning for a chance at a dream not so weighty or wild.

THE CHILDREN'S SCHOOL IN KATHMANDU

Before I left Hong Kong, Father Adam Gudalefsky, a Maryknoll priest, had given me the address of Mary and George Cheru, an Indian couple who were running a school for disabled children in Kathmandu. I wrote and asked if I might stay with them and work with the children for a few days, while I got acclimated to Nepal and worked out my agenda. They were happy to have some extra help, and George was at the airport when I arrived.

There were about twelve children with varying disabilities, ranging in age from four to fourteen. Thrilled at the sight of a new face, several of them gathered round for hugs and kisses. We played simple games till snacktime, then I brought out my guitar and sang them some tunes. They clapped and sang along while they ate their crackers, then I passed out a few harmonicas, some spoons and wooden drums, and we made our own symphony. How we sounded was of no concern. All that mattered was that everyone was totally involved in making it happen, and out of that came an energy that lifted all our spirits.

Students at the Children's School.

After our "symphony" was over, I brought out my Walkman with a tape of the Hong Kong Children's Chorus. I'll never forget the look on their faces as they each put on the headset and heard these children's voices ringing through their head. Suddenly their eyes widened, they stopped in their tracks and fixed their gaze straight ahead, like deer in the forest at the crack of a twig. Nothing else in their little world seemed to matter but the sound of this sweet singing, coming from a place they had never known.

As much fun as they had with the Walkman, their favorite activity was looking at Polaroid pictures. Mary sent word home with each of them one day that we'd be taking pictures the next day at school. They all showed up squeaky clean with their best clothes on and we spent the afternoon taking pictures of each other till the film ran out. They howled with delight when their photos came out of the little slot and could hardly wait the sixty seconds it took to develop the image. They were all so happy to go home that day, carrying little square pictures of themselves.

Despite the hassle of carrying all that equipment around, it made an incredible difference in the way I could relate to people. To watch their eyes light up when they heard the children's choir through a headset or to see their excitement at the pictures of themselves looking so happy – being able to share that much fun with those children made the extra effort worthwhile indeed.

After a week I left Mary and George's and went to find my old friend Sandie in Kathmandu. I had run into her in Bangkok and we agreed to meet in Nepal and trek together in the Himalayas. I finally tracked her down in a dingy hotel room, where she was sick with amoebic dysentery. There wasn't much we could do but wait it out, so she slept for a few days while I went to work at the Pashupatinah Temple for the Dying and Destitute.

In the Hindu tradition, one believes if you die at a temple your soul will go right to Vishnu. So the sisters of Mother Teresa's order have made a kind of hospice at the temple, to tend to the needs of those who've come to die. Mainly they clean their wounds, feed them rice and give them love. My work was the laundry detail. We washed all the sheets by hand, outdoors in the company of the temple monkeys and sacred cows.

One day when I was up to my shoulders in soapsuds and sheets, I looked across the courtyard and saw a most beautiful thing. A very old and crippled woman was giving a tender massage to a dying woman who couldn't move from her sickbed. She bathed her first, then took a tiny bottle of sweet smelling oil out of her little bag. For nearly an hour, she soothed and caressed the fragile body of her friend, then covered her with a clean sheet, took her hand and sat there quietly by her side.

To be there in the presence of that kind of giving, that kind of letting go, was more of a gift to me than those who were there will ever know.

Fruit Market Girl, Kathmandu, Nepal.

Peaceful Mountain Girl. I met her on a trail near Chandrakot. She was gathering wood with her sister, a job that consumes many hours of the day for children in Nepal. She asked if I had any pencils. I didn't, so I gave her my peace button instead. Though they know nothing of war in the Himalayas, hardship and hunger take their toll. As an average young woman, her life expectancy is forty-one years.

Finally made it to Kathmandu and am leaning out my window watching sacred cows meander to the sound of Willie Nelson. It's a golden Sunday morning in the lush green valley, with mountains stretching forever in every direction.

Kathmandu's an interesting city, a curious mingling of the seventeenth century and the jet age. Since trekking has become so popular (over a hundred hikers a day register for passes), there's been an outcrop of international restaurants serving haute cuisine to the hearty climbers. While hungry trekkers wind through the alleys in search of pizza, ice cream, brownies and burritos, holy cows with painted horns sashay down the streets as if they own the town. Kids play badminton with pebbles and cardboard and women stretch their six-foot saris from the rooftops to dry. On special occasions they wear nine-foot saris; hence, the expression "the whole nine yards."

There's a peaceful and accommodating blending of Hinduism and Buddhism, with shared deities, feasts and festivals. There are more gods and goddesses than I could ever remember, and more festivals than days of the year to honor them all. An interesting mix of spiritualities is demonstrated in the Kumari, the virgin goddess of Kathmandu. Though Kumari is a Hindu goddess, the living virgin goddess is a young girl, chosen from a Buddhist household, who lives in an ornately carved wooden structure with beautiful balconies and window screens. She appears on the balcony to wave to her devotees and, on special holidays, is transported through the town in a decorated chariot.

It's amazing to watch these rituals which have been going on for centuries, hundreds of years before Christ came along. Aside from a few temples where only Hindus are allowed, the Nepalis are thrilled to have people of all faiths participating in their religious festivities. Their entire lives are centered around their faith, with every day of the year a feast for one god or another. There is no catechism or particular dogma to subscribe to. No hard-nosed bickering about what's morally right or wrong. No petty conversations about one faith being better than another. No one day a week when people dress up, go to church and act bored in what they proclaim to be the presence of God.

Out of a population of fifteen million in Nepal, about ten thousand are Christians, of which about one thousand are Roman Catholic. I had dinner in a *rectory the other night and learned these things from the priests. There's a law against preaching for conversion, and one priest is now in jail because he was reported for performing a baptism. So the Christians here don't evangelize. They mainly do social work and set up schools and hospitals.*

King Birendra Bir Bikram Shah Deva is the tenth king in the Shah dynasty. He lives in a huge palace, "a fortress that maintains the separation between him and his people," according to Shambu, a Nepali university student I ate lunch with. "While many are starving and rummaging for food, he spends a lot of time taking trips in his royal helicopter. But what does he do for his people? Nothing."

The Nepalese are a docile people, though, and aside from some activity on the university campus, there are few signs of concern about the poverty that encumbers so many people. "No one thinks of trying to make a difference," said Shambu. "When some students spoke out last year about the the need for housing and food for the poor, the only result was that the king had a higher wall built around his palace. The people do not think about justice. If they are hungry, they try to get food, but they do not put blame anywhere for their hunger. It does not matter that people go hungry in this society."

Working for social justice in a Judeo-Christian context is fairly easy, because most people agree with the basic premise that all people should have equal access to a healthy and comfortable life. In a Hindu culture, however, no such premise underlies their faith. Inequality and suffering are explained by karma, the force generated by a person's actions in a previous lifetime that determines her/his destiny in this one. Hindus accept the situation they are born into and do their best to fulfill the duties required of them within its confines, be they beggars, servants or priests. Changing the social structure to achieve equality and justice would be an absurd idea for the Hindu, because carefully delineated social roles and karmic appreciation are integral aspects of their faith.

Standing in the presence of poverty and trying to perceive it as part of the perfect order of the universe is difficult for me at this time. Maybe I will grow into a deeper appreciation of this worldview and will cease being haunted by the desire to bring my form of comfort to every person's life.

— JOURNAL ENTRY

NEW LESSONS AT LINCOLN SCHOOL

Through a friend, I met a woman who taught at the International School in Kathmandu, a school for all the American and English-speaking students who are children of U.S. personnel working in Nepal. I asked if I might show *Focus on Peace* and make a presentation to the students. She said she'd check with the principal and let me know.

The principal and a few teachers wanted to preview the slideshow to be sure it wasn't "subversive." I was sure they'd love it since I'd received nothing but affirmation everywhere I showed it. The only changes I'd made were at the request of a Japanese A-bomb survivor who asked if I'd include a few photos from Hiroshima taken shortly after the bomb was dropped. Since the students in Nepal have no television and only limited access to radio, I thought it was important that they see those slides to better understand the context of the peace movement and the seriousness of the issues involved.

I was caught off guard by the negative response of the principal, who said the slideshow "failed to address the issues, was propagandist and the children shouldn't be exposed to it." One teacher asked if I was for unilateral or bilateral disarmament, a discussion I hated to enter into because it put issues into an intellectual realm when my work is to encourage people to take the questions into their hearts.

I reminded the teacher that I was traveling as an artist, using my images to inspire thought and communication on a deeper level, not to debate about political or military issues. I was there to fill in details about a growing movement for peace in the United States, a movement that people rarely read or hear about because the press does not cover it. I was there to say that this movement, too, is going on, along with the massive defense spending and military buildup that the international press *does* report. I wanted them to know that thousands of people in the United States and Canada are saying that it is time to put an end to war, to resolve our conflicts in other ways, to use our resources for the benefit of humankind, not for our destruction.

Of course it's not clear to us yet how to resolve global conflicts in peaceful ways – nor will it *ever* be clear, in my opinion, unless we first commit ourselves to creating peace. Only then will the grace, the wisdom and the courage arrive to help us design the blueprint we need for global reconciliation.

The science teacher who'd asked about disarmament became very upset and started talking about the Russians taking over the world. "You must love the Russians!" he shouted, his fists in the air. "I do my best to love all people," I said. "Then," he replied, "you should go there where you belong!" The other teachers argued among themselves whether the students had "anything to learn" from seeing the slideshow, while I stood there numbed by the chill in the room.

They finally decided that I could make a presentation to the seventh, eighth and ninth graders, but that someone from the "opposition" would debate me at the end, so the kids could get the whole picture. The teachers took the next day to prep the students and I spent the day in quiet reflection.

The next morning I took a cab out to Lincoln School, noticing nothing but the knots in my stomach all the way there. At nine o'clock, I talked with the students about the images they'd be seeing. I also talked about why I was there and told them how much I believe in the power of their creative imaginations. They were attentive and full of life, and each one felt like a kindred spirit.

Many were in tears after the slides, some moved by horror and some by hope. The room was very still and we agreed to take a twenty-minute break before the debate.

When the time came, we sat in a big circle on the floor, with the science teacher directly across from me. I asked if any of the students would like to share their feelings about what they had seen, what's going on in the world and how we're dealing with it as global citizens. After a few had spoken about their fear of war, the science teacher started to talk about the dangerous Russians and how important it is that we can win a war with them if they threaten to take over our country.

"No, don't you see?" asked one student. "We cannot afford to make a war anymore for any reason. The weapons we have are so dangerous they will kill too many people and even kill our planet."

Another student agreed. "Something new has to happen now. We have to make up a new way of fighting. The old way can't work anymore."

The teacher was challenged by the students in a loving way, with profound insights and brilliant questions. Eventually he grew silent as the dialogue moved from the mind to the heart. He listened carefully to everything they had to say as they raised their hands and shared their feelings. At the end of the session, he shared these feelings with the group. "I have come to understand something very important here today and it has to do with what we believe. All my life I've held to the beliefs I grew up with. Because I learned certain things from my father, my ministers, my teachers, I trusted that they were right – and I think they probably were for their time. What I learned today is that things are very different now. It is not the same world and the old answers no longer work. I cannot tell you that I think we should destroy all our weapons and go to Russia with no defense, trusting in their goodness. But I do agree that we shouldn't continue to build weapons that could very well destroy the world and risk the chance of them getting in the wrong hands. So thank you for being the bright young thinkers that you are and for making a difference in my life today."

The students clapped and cheered and the science teacher walked over to shake my hand. "Best of luck on the rest of your journey," he said with a smile. "You too," I said and went on my way, thankful for life's amazing graces.

BEYOND THE BEYONDS:
INTO THE HEART OF THE HIMALAYAS

When Sandie recovered her health, we bought our maps, determined our itinerary and registered for a trek to the Annapurna Base Camp, a two-week climb up to 14,000 feet.

The first few days were torturous. For nine or ten hours a day we trekked and trudged, sweating through our clothes and halfway through our packs, hardly speaking, just following the trail up and down mountains that were almost vertical. My mind resisted as much as my body, obsessed by the pain, regretting the decision, wanting to turn back and forget the whole idea. All I could think about was the weight on my back, and I felt like I was climbing up Golgotha.

Villages were few and far between, so it was always near dark by the time we reached the tea houses, sleeping cabins along the trails that provided food and lodging for a dollar

Rhododendron forest in the Himalayas.

Blue Mountain Woman. She passed me on a narrow mountain path, walking
barefoot with a huge load of wood. When she stopped for a cigarette at 10,000
feet, there was hardly enough oxygen to keep it lit. We rested awhile together and
then I helped her with her bamboo pack. She was like my grandmother, and I
watched her walk five miles up a mountain carrying a pack I could hardly lift.

a day. We'd have our bowl of rice and vegetables, a cup of tea, then right to bed, our knees still shaky from the rigorous workout.

On the morning of the fourth day, when I looked out the window, I saw a view I could hardly believe. Right there before me stood the highest, most magnificent mountains I had ever seen. Purple and mauve in the morning light, their snow-covered peaks pierced the clouds, reaching forever into the sky's blue heights. There was Machhapuchhare, Gangapurna, Fang, Glacier Dome, Hiunchuli, the Annapurnas, Roc Noir – ranging from 21,000 to 26,545 feet high.

I couldn't wait to get going that day. Even my pack felt lighter when I picked it up. Having the peaks in sight made all the difference, and my whole being shifted into the zen of the climb. It no longer mattered whether I was ascending or descending, whether the path was steep or carving its way through a rhododendron forest. Once I stopped thinking about the pain, my mind became free enough to be nowhere and there was nothing going on but the slow, steady movement of one foot after another.

The day was beautiful and we'd been climbing for hours. I was on the edge of a cliff, peering down at the layers of hills that stretched for miles far below when huge black clouds rolled in, coloring the sky a charcoal gray. An awesome silence filled the air. As far as I could see, there were no people around and all signs of life had disappeared. The cows were gone, no dogs were barking and not a birdsong could be heard. "This is it," I thought. "The world is coming to an end and here I am in the middle of the Himalayas. What do I do now?"

Sandie had gone ahead, full of energy while I stopped for a break, and I suddenly felt more alone than I had ever been before. A bolt of thunder cracked the silence and I ran up the path, searching for refuge. By now the rain was beating down and I could barely see the muddy trail. Breathless and soaking, I kept on moving till a flash of yellow caught my eye. It was Sandie in her yellow jacket, sharing the shelter of a tree with some frightened cows.

I stumbled down to where she was sitting and we huddled together against the storm. Not knowing whether to stay or go, we sat for a while and waited for help.

"Sandie," I said, breaking the silence, "I think I hear a voice."

"Oh yeah? What kind of voice?" she asked, staring ahead at the nervous cows.

"You know, an inner voice," I said sheepishly.

"An inner voice," she repeated. "Good, and what is it saying?"

"It's saying we should keep going," I replied.

"Keep going?" she asked, as a streak of lightning whitewashed the landscape. "Now? Keep going now?" she quizzed.

"Yeah, now. Before it gets worse."

She turned toward me making sure this was not a joke. "O.K., then, let's get going," she said, grabbing a low limb and hoisting herself up. We snapped up our jackets, tightened our hoods, and crawled back up to the flooding path.

It wasn't long before the rain stopped and a hazy mist enshrouded our world. We hadn't walked far when, rounding a bend, we came upon an old Tibetan man thatching a roof on the edge of a cliff. He waved us over, motioning for us to sit down beside him.

Within moments, the sun broke through in radiant streams, turning the valley below into a chasm of color. Rainbows bounced off dewy boulders and the peaks ahead were bathed in gold. The three of us sat in total silence, bonded somehow by the beauty before us.

No one moved until his wife called out and waved us into their tiny hut where she was cooking rice on an open fire and brewing up some tea for us.

When we came in soaked and muddy, she sat us down by the fire to dry, then spread our jackets out on the rocks. While we drank tea out of battered tin cups, the wife stirred the rice with her small, bare hands while her husband whittled the end of a bamboo shoot. Then he took an old cigarette out of a small metal box, fit it neatly into his new bamboo holder, and passed it to me after lighting it up.

We smoked and laughed and talked with our hands, sharing what we could of the joy in our hearts. Then when it was time to go, they walked us back to the steaming trail and stood there waving till we were out of sight.

Arriving at the Annapurna Base Camp was like reaching the promised land. It was late when we got there and freezing cold, so I bundled up, put on my hat, mittens and extra socks and jumped into my sleeping bag. Half a dozen others sat around the fire, drinking tea and telling stories in Nepali and French, but I was too tired to stay up and enjoy the camaraderie. We were at 14,000 feet and the wind howled fiercely all night long through the loosely woven slats of our bamboo hut. There were no beds, only little mats on the cold, dirt floor and no doors to keep out the elements. I woke up that morning with snow on my face.

At four o'clock, I rose for the climb I'd been waiting for: another hour's journey up into the sanctuary, where I could watch the sunrise in the presence of forty of Mother Earth's tallest peaks. On the way up, a thunderous avalanche on Machhapuchhare covered the entire mountainside with a cloud of snow. All else was silent in the crisp early hours.

Sitting there on the ridge before those mighty and ancient mountains filled me with such awe that I started to weep. I cried awhile, feeling so lucky, so full of joy. Then I prayed. And sang. And cried some more. I was not the same person who had almost turned back several days before, thinking that the journey was far too hard. I could never describe in words the impact of being there in the center of that majesty, in the arms of my Mother, this holy earth. The imprint of that moment is forever with me, the source of great peace in unsettling times.

LEFT: The storm approaches.

BELOW: Sherpas take a rest during the long climb.

I'm stretched out on a rock like a lazy salamander, sunning myself and waiting for my clothes to dry. We made it to 9,000 feet and ran into a beautiful waterfall and swimming hole halfway up the mountain. The climbs have been exhausting, as hard on the knees going down as going up. By the end of the day, after nine hours of climbing, my legs won't stop shaking for over an hour.

The Nepali women put me to shame with their strength and stamina. While I'm bent over like a hunchback on these crooked trails, trying to manage thirty-five pounds, they come ripping past in their little bare feet with eighty pounds of rice on their backs. Huge muletrains pass us by about twice a day, carrying goods for those who can pay. The poorer mountain dwellers must carry their own.

Supplies are minimal at 9,000 feet. No toilets, no mirrors, no beds, no beer, and the same food for breakfast, lunch and dinner. Fried rice, boiled rice, rice with egg, rice with veggies, and for dessert, a special treat — rice pudding. There's even a homemade rice hooch called rakshi that takes my mind off my pain in a matter of minutes.

I'm taking lots of photographs because no words could really convey what it's like to be up here. It's kind of silenced me in a way, awesome as it is. When I see how hard these people work and how simply they live their lives, it touches me in a place where words don't live.

Yesterday I passed a French man who was heading up to Annapurna. He had a guide with him, but he was carrying all his own gear. When I was behind them, I wondered why they were going so slowly. It wasn't till I passed by and waved hello that I noticed he was blind. A lot changed for me then, knowing he was right behind, with obstacles more difficult than any of my own.

Being in the Himalayas is changing me in many ways — slowing me down, displacing my fears, bringing me closer to the Great Source of it all. As exhausting as it is physically, it's spiritually exhilarating. I feel like I'm expanding somehow … my dimensions are deeper, more solid and stable. Like maybe I'm growing in the right direction ….

— JOURNAL ENTRY

Rangpur, India.

HUMAN DEVELOPMENT, INDIA-STYLE

My first experience in India was a visit to an integrated Hindu-Muslim-Christian community in Muzaffarpur, Bihar, an area where the poorest 7 percent of the world's population lives. A friend in Nepal gave me the name of Bill Christensen, a Marianist priest whose commitment to the poor led to his role in the establishment of Paroo Prakhand Samagra Vikas Pariyojna, the Paroo Block Integrated Development Project. PPSVP is an effort to set up a model development for the area of 330 million people of northeast India and Bangladesh. For this purpose, 137 villages comprising 180,000 people were chosen to motivate and organize the people in such a way that they could be independent of outside assistance after eight to ten years.

"The main goal of the project," said Christensen, "is to create unity and justice where there is none and to establish equality between people," a difficult task given India's socially complex caste system and its Muslim-Hindu rift. Eleven Hindus, two Muslims, and one Christian make up the core staff. These twelve men and two women, who live together in the village area, are working to build a strong community among themselves and hope this will be a model for the villagers.

"We're ready to take a stand for the poor and to give rights to women, despite criticism from the village," asserted Christensen. "We're here for justice, which we hope will lead people to compassion. Though it's the duty of society to provide opportunity for human development for each member, at PPSVP we believe that it's the responsibility of each person to be concerned for the common good and community spirit of all members of their society. Our work is to provide opportunities for poor people's uplift in the context of unity and fellowship."

As a result of its colonial history, India missed out on the Industrial Revolution, entering the modern world in 1947 at a tremendous economic disadvantage. In the district of Muzaffarpur, 90 percent of the people have agriculture as their occupation, though 60 percent are landless, 37 percent have between one and ten acres, and only 3 percent have over ten acres of land. Except for a few cities, the area lacks electricity, good roads, sanitation, educational and health facilities.

People live in twenty-dollar grass and bamboo huts, with six to eight people crowding into an eight by ten foot space. Eighty percent of the people are illiterate. The per capita annual income is only thirty to forty dollars because of landlessness, unemployment and low wages. All of them have parasites living in their stomachs and are both malnourished and undernourished. They never see a doctor or visit a hospital and only use simple village remedies to deal with the most serious of diseases, such as typhoid, cholera, dysentery, tuberculosis and malaria.

PPSVP has organized programs to deal with all aspects of human development. They have training programs for employment, health care, agriculture, education, sanitation and

Sewing class in the Karmwari-Musahal Tola.

community building. They operate five schools for children, though they can only accommodate one child from each family because of limited space and teachers. Since the illiteracy rate among women is 95 percent in their area, higher than the rate for men, the school enrolls 60 percent girls and 40 percent boys – one small step for womankind. Some of the classes PPSVP offers adults include ropemaking, sandal making and repair, beekeeping, hand loom weaving, tailoring, tree nurseries and fruit preservation. They have trained 30 women for the Mother-Child Health Care Program which has helped 3600 families.

I went to a sewing class with about fifteen village women, each of whom had two or three small children in tow. Women took turns learning to use the two sewing machines, while they swatted flies and tended to their babies. The temperature that day was 110 degrees.

The project follows the principle of *antyoda*ya, meaning that the poorest and most deprived members of the society must be given first preference in development. Many of the people they are serving are the untouchables, India's lowest caste – the ones Mahatma Gandhi called *harijans,* or children of God. I visited one community referred to as the

Karmwari-Musahal Tola, which means "the rat-eaters." These people have so little that they look for rat's nests so they can kill and eat the rodents, then take what grain the rats have stored. The harijans have no land of their own and dozens of them live crowded together into small huts.

When I asked Bill about his perceptions of the caste system, he was both respectful of the religion and cultural traditionand clear about its drawbacks:

> While we work to change the social and economic order and bring about more distributive justice in this community, we also try to enrich the caste system, helping people to develop their cultural heritage. But these traditions are very old and people find it hard to think any other way....

LEFT: Awadhesh Kumar Singh showers at the pump.

RIGHT: Woman from village Phulwaria.

They've been taught all their lives not to have any contact with the harijans, yet now we're trying to teach classes that are open to all castes. I had a young boy's uncle come by here yesterday saying he didn't want his nephew learning hand loom from a Muslim, even though learning a new trade might be the only hope for that boy. It's so divisive. People identify with their caste members regardless of right or wrong, and political leaders exploit the castes to win votes.

You can't help but be angry at the exploitation of the poor that is going on, but anger is not violence. It is more violent to sit passively by and let the violence of exploitation continue.

We often receive criticism for our work at integration, and I've learned the hard way that identifying with the poor means being powerless and being opposed by powerful people. But we keep on in the face of it all, striving for the unity we're all committed to.

The fourteen members who live at the project have frequent seminars, picnics, monthly gatherings and shared prayer, called *satsang*, which means "truth and community." When I asked Bill about their spirituality, he said, "We don't work at our spirituality, but share it as each one wants to. We try to grow together in our commitment to the poor, and we bring a tremendous variety of commitments as a group. The people of Paroo are not only learning new information; they are also learning to overcome the divisions in their fragmented society which have prevented them from creating a community and becoming self-reliant. Through our work here, women sit together equally with men, Muslims sit together equally with Hindus, and harijans sit together equally with the backward and forward castes to decide their future. This is a people's movement for development and the real living out of our religion."

After a few days at Paroo Prakhand, I was in a rickshaw heading back to Patna and all the comforts of a Jesuit seminary. As I passed by the villagers who were building and planting together in the early morning light, they waved and called out their warm goodbyes. "Yes," I thought, "they've got it right. This is what religion really ought to look like."

I've been in India four days and have been deathly ill with intestinal sickness ever since I went through customs. Delhi Belly, they call it, and only the chosen few are spared its touch.

I'm visiting a development project in Muzaffarpur, a sixty-mile trip from Patna that took six gruelling hours. Being a foreigner and such an oddity in these parts, I managed to get a seat on the bus, but had to share it with two women and four kids. Rusty springs were poking through the tattered seatcovers and every bump meant another poke. With all this going on in 110-degree heat, I felt like I was being tortured in a bouncing oven.

Once the bus finally got to the village, I had to find a rickshaw driver who could understand the directions I had written on a little scrap of paper. And I thought the bus ride was difficult! Thirty minutes later, I was in the middle of the street, ready to give up, when a kind merchant came over to see if he could help. Being one of the few educated villagers, he deciphered the note, found a driver and loaded my bags into a bicycle rickshaw.

I was horrified when I saw my driver, who was about thirty years my senior and forty pounds lighter. How could I sit there while he pedaled me and all my heavy bags down bumpy dirt roads for three miles? I asked the merchant if there were any motorized rickshaws in town and he said no.

With no other choices, we started out, and I sat behind my little driver, watching the muscles ripple around his spindly legs and the sweat run like rain off his bony bare back. "Stop!" I yelled out at one point. Please let me pedal for a while." He didn't understand a word I was saying, but when I pointed at me on the seat and him in the back, shook his head no. "No, no," he kept saying, as he hopped back on his seat and took off down the dusty trail.

After an hour, he pulled into the project, making a final sprint right for the pump. He drenched himself with cool water and looked surprised when I followed suit, pouring a whole bucketful over my head. By this time the temperature was 115 degrees and I felt like my fever was catching up.

– JOURNAL ENTRY

Black Shawl Woman. One of the "untouchables," a member of India's lowest caste. She invited me to her hut for tea. It had two rooms and there were 14 people who lived there.

It was Easter Sunday and I awoke from my dreams longing to hear the Hallelujah Chorus. The temperature was 120 degrees, the monsoon was approaching and a cholera epidemic was ripping through the city, taking hundreds of lives each day. As I walked the steamy streets looking for signs of life and resurrection, I found these kids cleaning up and having a ball at the public bath, their only source of water. When I stopped to photograph them, I heard from a little church across the street the final strains of the Hallelujah Chorus.

EASTER IN CALCUTTA

After a few weeks in northern India, I met up with my friend Sandie who had been travelling in Bhutan since we left Nepal. We met on Good Friday at the Salvation Army Red Shield Guest House, a dingy hotel with hungry bedbugs, broken fans and showers that worked only twice a day. Having come from a few days at a quiet Jesuit seminary, the chaos of Calcutta was almost too much to bear.

Hordes of crippled beggars approached me at the station, all tugging at my clothes for a few precious rupees. I was still sick with dysentery, and it was all I could do to drag my gear after a twenty-hour train ride on a hard wooden bench. The beggars' insistent pawing in that crowded terminal turned the feverish day into a Fellini nightmare. What might have led to compassion in a healthier moment now drove me closer to the ragged edge.

Tears streaked my face as I trudged through the maze of broken bodies, horrified in the presence of so much tragedy. I made my way to an empty corner, then sat on the floor with my head in my hands and cried till the pain was released. Then I gathered my pieces and started again.

Once outside, I had to haggle forever with the rickshaw drivers who wanted me to pay dearly for a trip across town. I knew it should cost between 20 and 40 rupees, but the best offer I was getting was 100. I settled for 50 in the sweltering heat and was soon dropped off at the Red Shield's door.

The first two days I spent in bed, only getting up for a trip to the shower. It was hard to sleep with the bedbugs biting, so I rose at dawn for the rooftop service on Easter Sunday. There were six chubby Indians dressed in Salvation Army uniforms and seven motley travellers who looked as bedraggled as I.

We sang a few militant hymns like "Onward Christian Soldiers," listened to a Bible passage, and the next thing I knew it was the last amen. On the way downstairs, a scraggly American invited me to an opium den he'd just heard about. "No thanks," I said. "What I really want a hit of is a church choir singing the Hallelujah Chorus." I checked out my map and found two churches, but got there at the end of both services.

At the first one, a Roman Catholic Church, I heard the final chorus and the last alleluias from half a block away where I'd stopped to take pictures of kids in the street. The second one was an Episcopal Cathedral and I arrived as all the well-dressed people were shaking hands and leaving the church. The smell of incense drew me in and the still burning candles made me feel at home. I sunk into a pew that wrapped around me like half a sarcophagus, listening to the organist finish "Jesu, Joy of Man's Desiring." She played a few more songs before the lights went out, giving me a chance to celebrate Easter in my own quiet way.

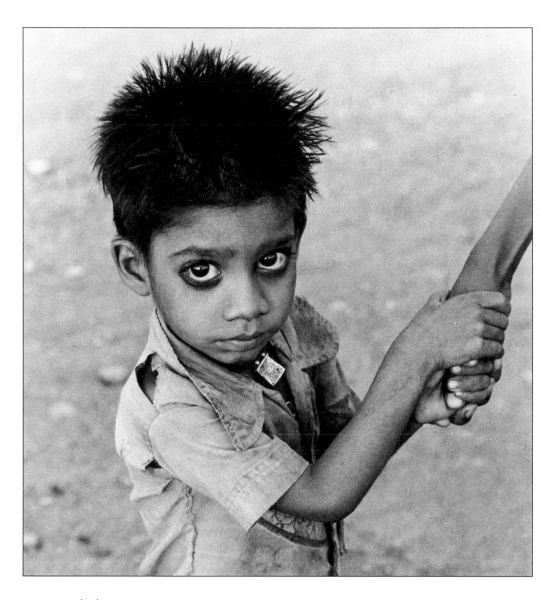

There's days the weight of this journey cracks my back, lays me down on a cold bed of sorrow, the comforter gone. Why am I doing this? Why this need to look at the inner lining? What am I trying to learn that I don't already know? I've never been in a place that's such a mirror to the soul, reflecting the poverty of spirit as much as the wealth of it. Nothing seems to make any sense. I'm beginning to understand that little of India has to do with reason, at least as we define it in the West.

— JOURNAL ENTRY

JOURNEY TO AUROVILLE, THE CITY OF PEACE

Before I left Syracuse, I was looking through an encyclopedia of alternative communities and came across a place called Auroville, located in southern India. It was referred to as a City of Peace and described as an experiment in international understanding and personal and social transformation. With five hundred residents, it boasted of a community that transcended politics, nationalities and religions in its attempt to achieve human unity. Intrigued with the possibility of such a place this side of Eden, I decided to go there. Auroville was the one Indian location I had on my agenda when I began the trip.

Reading about Auroville in a moderate climate was a lot more seductive than trying to get there during the monsoon season at peak travel time. It took a few days from Calcutta, heading south to Pondicherry, with stops along the way for sanity and reality checks. The crowds were not to be believed, and every decent hotel along the way had been booked weeks in advance by smart vacationers. Sandie had decided to come along before heading for Kashmir, so at least we had each other to blame when everything went wrong.

After a sleepless night in Madras in a sleazy, roach-ridden room, we made a pact to stay on the train till it got to Pondicherry. The next night we spent bruising our hips on the hard wooden bunks, as the train rattled on through the dark heat of night.

It was 6:00 A.M. when the whistle blew, announcing our arrival in the quaint little town. We drank sweet coffee in a crowded cafe, then I stayed with the packs while Sandie went for information. A few minutes later, she was back with a map to Auroville and the name of a place where we could rent some bikes. Then we found a room, took a quick shower and made our plans. We had to ride about six miles south, so we headed right out before the sun got too hot. After a few wrong turns and several misguided directions, we pedalled our way into a flowering oasis. Here in the middle of a red clay desert was Auroville, a sweet-smelling garden of delight.

Sandie went one way and I another, agreeing to meet in Pondicherry when we were finished exploring. I passed by a variety of interesting structures – windmills, solar homes, habitable treehouses, bamboo cabins, white stucco apartments. There seemed no end to the architectural diversity. When I finally saw a man out in the field, I walked out to ask for some information.

He explained that Auroville covered about twenty square miles and that I was in the area where they were experimenting with irrigation projects, land reclamation, afforestation and renewable energy systems. Engineers and environmentalists from Europe, Australia and the United States were working with Indian villagers to see what they could produce from the barren environment. Too busy to talk long, he sent me off in another direction, to the information office in the center of the community.

On my way, I met an American named Jocelyn who was riding down the road on a battered blue motorcycle. She had lived there ten years and had started a shoe-making cooperative that now employed twenty-five village women. They crocheted shoes which were exported and sold in exclusive American stores. "Follow me through this field and I'll show you where I live," she yelled, as she kicked it into gear and took off down the trail. I pedalled as fast as I could through the bamboo forest, ready to collapse when I got to her home, a spacious, round thatched hut in the middle of paradise. "Sit over there, while I get some tea," she said, pointing to a huge hammock suspended from the ceiling. I caught my breath while she brewed up our drinks and filled me in on the history of the area.

Auroville is founded on the work of one of India's modern visionaries, Sri Aurobindo, who retreated to Pondicherry after years of intense involvement in the struggle for independence. It was there he envisioned a new humanity, based on the possibility of spiritual/ cellular transformation and the emergence of a supramental consciousness.

In 1920, he was joined by an exceptional French woman, Mirra Richard, who came to be known later as simply "the Mother." Both of them were engaged in opening new avenues for human development, aiming, in Sri Aurobindo's words, "not to found a religion or a school of philosophy or a school of yoga, but to create a ground of spiritual growth and experience which will bring down a greater Truth beyond mind, but not inaccessible to the human soul and consciousness." They were both prolific writers who expressed their ideas in several major philosophical and spiritual works.

After Sri Aurobindo's death, it was under the Mother's guidance that the city of peace began to take shape. On February 28, 1968, young people representing 124 nations each placed a handful of their country's earth in a lotus-shaped marble urn. This was the symbolic start of Auroville, a city which now includes over 40 settlements and 500 permanent residents from more than 20 nations. Their common commitment is to change human consciousness, and their work is an attempt to create a spiritual and material environment that will hasten humanity's evolutionary development.

I knew I had to stay there for a while and asked if there were accomodations for visitors. "Oh, sure," she said. "I'll lead you over to the main office and you can register for temporary housing." Within a couple of hours, I'd worked out the details and was riding back to Pondicherry to meet Sandie, who had also decided to spend a little time there after meeting some residents and looking around.

Auroville is a totally self-sustaining operation, with schools, offices, a library, an auditorium, music rooms, a mechanics center, huge gardens, community dining halls, a printing operation and several cottage industries providing work for the local villagers who have been integrated into the community.

One of the most impressive structures, still under construction, is the Matrimandir, "the soul of Auroville," which the Mother envisioned as "a place for trying to find one's consciousness. There are no fixed meditations. The people spend their time there in silence and concentration."

A huge sphere, standing a hundred feet tall, the Matrimandir is supported by four pillars reaching deep into the earth. Inside the supporting structure is a twelve-sided chamber. At the top is an opening to receive and channel a ray of light from the sun. This beam of light is directed into the center of the sanctuary through a tracking mirror, flows through a crystal suspended in a hole cut through the floor, then travels down into a pool of water at the base and is reflected back again.

All the work is being done by hand, from the building of the forms to the mixing of the cement, so it will take many years before the dream is finished. I spent a few days on the construction crew, mixing stones and sand for hours at a time with several Aurovillians who are committed to its completion. When lunchtime came, about twenty-five workers gathered together and food was biked in from the nearest dining hall. Conversations were taking place in several languages, including French, Dutch, Italian, English and Hindi. Strangely enough, I felt right at home.

I usually worked in the morning and spent the afternoons reading and visiting with Seyril, a sixty-five-year-old playwright from Colorado who had come to Auroville in 1968. The library was full of Aurobindo's and the Mother's works, so I read intently for hours at a time. These two figures and their work were held in the highest esteem. One night I went to a reading of some of Mother's poetry. She taped most of her work before she died, so it was her own voice we were hearing. I understood little of it, since she had a very intense accent and I wasn't familiar with the work, but the power of the event I'll never forget.

There were only about twelve of us, gathered together in a candle-lit room with open arched windows and an age-old ambience. As Mother's deep voice came to life in our pres-

ence, the candle flames danced in the warm evening breeze, as if keeping time with her poetic rhythm. Our shadows came alive on the white stucco wall, given wings by the vibrant flame, though no one was moving while the reading went on.

We stopped to sit on the circular steps that spiraled around the earth-filled urn, which appeared like a chalice beneath the full moon host. There in the shadow of the Matrimandir, we held each other's hand and gave thanks to the Mother who had filled our hearts and thanks to each other for being so alive. Then Seyril took me to her little room and gave me her tape of Paul Winter's *Missa Gaia,* which I listened to for hours while I watched the shooting stars from my bamboo treehouse.

Marble urn filled with soil from 124 nations.

The Matrimandir under construction.

Everyone here is so busy building and working on their own lives, they don't spend much time being together. I love how the community is physically set up, but I miss a sense of bondedness among the people who live here. It seems to lack a culture of its own, though it's hard for me to say after just a week.

I've been spending a lot of time with Seyril. We've gone everywhere on our bikes and she's introduced me to people from all over the world. There are more visionaries per square foot than I ever thought possible — scientists, artists, engineers, architects, writers, environmentalists — all immersed in their own creative projects, from working with windmills to working with dreams.

The children I've met seem very bright and have a wide variety of schools and educational options. The other day I ran into my little friend Akash, an eight-year-old from Holland who's lived here all his life. He was with an older villager who was busy working on a broken pump. "Hi, Akash," I said. "How come you're not in school?" Akash glanced at me with a look of impatience. "Don't you know," he said, his arms crossed and eyebrows arched, "this is my school."

– JOURNAL ENTRY

ANAND NIKETAN — A GANDHIAN ASHRAM

When I was in Thailand, I joined an organization called SERVAS, a cooperative system of international hosts and travelers established to help build world peace by providing opportunities for personal contacts among people of different cultures. It is a non-profit, nonpolitical, interracial and interfaith network in which foreign visitors are invited to share life in the home and community of the host for two to three days without cost. Its goal is to allow opportunities for people of diverse nationalities to share their concerns about social and international problems, their interests in creative activity and their mutual responsibility for humankind.

As I was looking through the list of hosts in India, I saw a Gandhian Ashram called Anand Niketan, meaning Abode of Joy. I wrote to the director, Harivallabh Parikh, and asked if I could come for a visit. When I arrived in Calcutta, his letter of invitation was waiting for me, so I made my way to Gujarat without delay.

An ashram worker met me at the train station and took me to Mr. Parikh's house in Baroda, where his family was making preparations to go to the ashram the next day. Mr. Parikh, who insisted I call him Bhai, which means "brother" in Hindi, introduced me to his wife Prabhaben, his two daughters, Yogina and Tapsi, and three grandchildren who were visiting his home.

The women fed me immediately and Bhai started telling the story of his life with Gandhi. Bhai was born in 1924 into an aristocratic family of feudal lords and came under the influence of the nationalist guests who frequented his father's house. At the age of fourteen, he was introduced to Mahatma Gandhi and was so moved by the man that he left his family to study with Gandhi in the ashram at Wardha, then on to the Gujarat Vidyapeeth ashram. At the master's side, he learned the theory and practice of the nonviolent struggle for a just society rooted in love and generosity. Gandhi strongly encouraged his followers to dedicate themselves to India's villages, where 85 percent of the population lives.

During the partition era, when terrible battles were being fought between Hindus and Muslims over the newly established boundaries, Bhai was badly beaten by armed soldiers when he tried to protect some Muslims from being killed. To this day, he must keep his neck covered with a headcloth and wear a back brace to relieve the pain.

Bhai was twenty-five when Mahatma Gandhi was assassinated in January of 1949. Eleven months later, Bhai took his leader's advice, went to the isolated tribal area of Rangpur, settled under a neem tree and began his work, expecting that he would teach the people to spin cotton.

The Rathva Koli and Bhil tribes, also known as Adivasis, lived in this area and were working hard to eke a living out of the dry, inhospitable hill tracts. Most had lost their land to corrupt moneylenders, who charged 100 to 300 percent interest on loans to the Adivasis. Notorious for their short tempers and violent ways, the tribal people used violence to settle disputes. At the time Bhai and his wife arrived, there were three to four deaths a week due to family quarrels.

Though the moneylenders had warned the Adivasis not to get involved with this new couple, a few of them took their complaints to Bhai, who acted as a referee and settled many of the complaints amicably. This was the beginning of his Lok Adalat, the Open People's Court, which has settled more than eighty thousand civil and criminal disputes in the last four decades.

"When we go tomorrow," Bhai promised, "you will be surprised to see what we have accomplished since 1949. Life has changed dramatically for the Adivasis, who are now maintaining the machines, keeping the accounts, setting up irrigation systems, organizing cooperatives and planning together for the future."

The next day, we packed up the jeep and headed out for the three-hour journey to Anand Niketan, where I lived and worked for the next two weeks.

Yogina, Helli and Prabhaben, daughter, grand-daughter and wife of Bhai.

BHAI'S REFLECTIONS ON ANAND NIKETAN

One afternoon, I sat down with Bhai, a tape recorder and a list of questions I had about the history of the ashram. Here are some of his reflections:

I learned many things from Mahatma Gandhi, but the main thing was how to live a simple life, how to give importance to labor, how to love labor. Because the distance between poor and rich is so great, Gandhi taught us to identify with the laborer, who is thought to be less important. The one who is sitting at the table, using the pen, counting money – he is always thought to be more important.

When Gandhi decided to close this gap between the poor and the rich – he never used the words communism or socialism, but he was a communist in the real sense, in the sense of commune, in the biblical sense of the word – he started by grinding the wheel. Village people are poorer than town people, and town people are poorer than city people. In villages, those without land are poorer than those with land, but the women of the village are the poorest of them all – and that's why Gandhi took up what women were doing.

When a woman starts her daily work, she begins at four in the morning grinding flour for the whole family, grinding and sweating for two hours. So Gandhi started grinding to identify with the poorest sector of society. Once you identify with people, you don't feel their problems are your subjects. Their problems become your problems, their troubles become your troubles.

There are very many people, good writers, good speakers who speak in a language that makes the people cry and the listener would think how much this person has heart for the poor people. But some only play with the words, they have no identification with the problems of the poor. So Gandhi started with this and he always identified himself with the people he wanted to serve.

I learned from Gandhi that the people needed economic and social freedom as well as political freedom, and I am working with the Adivasis on four fronts: harassment of the tribal peoples, corruption and exploitation with the money-lenders, production and cultivation problems due to ignorance, and overproduction in population.

To overcome corruption, I've started a cooperative movement to provide loans at reasonable rates. Before, when people were trying to pay 300 percent interest, they always lost their land to the moneylender because they could not pay. The moneylenders then became the landlords. But to abuse the moneylender and landlords doesn't solve the problem. Gandhian philosophy says you must provide the alternative. Gandhi always said: "If you believe that this man is doing wrong, then you start doing what you feel is right. If you're doing right, then other people will know he is doing wrong and you are doing right. Instead of fighting with him, you correct yourself. If you are right, people will follow you."

Once people come up economically and socially, education follows and then politics. The government, most of the time, tries to do the right thing with the wrong methods and that is why it does not succeed. Here we are doing things not with force, but through training, teaching, showing people what is in their interest. That is the real way of Gandhian thought, *hryaday parivatan*, the change of heart.

I came here to get my country complete freedom, yet I am not ashamed to tell you, we are on the bank of it. We have not crossed the bank and perhaps many more years we will have to continue the work to get complete freedom. If one can earn bread without doing an hour's work, and another cannot earn bread after working hard twelve hours, how can you define this as a democratic country?

When I see that there is very little suffering, when people can enjoy whatever they want, when everybody gets an opportunity to become what they want, only then will I feel like my country has advanced in the proper direction and proportions.

Bhai

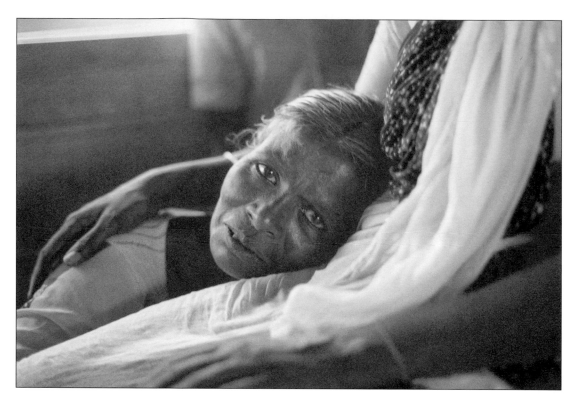

Mother at daughter's knee.

The other day I was on a train, riding in the Ladies' Compartment with four women and three children. We had plenty of room, and when another woman appeared in the doorway looking for a seat, I motioned for her to come in. The other women seemed perturbed and they all turned the other way and looked out the window. The woman in the doorway did not come in.

I didn't know what was going on, but something seemed strange. When I asked the woman next to me why they didn't move over, she said something about her being Muslim. I got up then and motioned for the woman to please take my seat. She was hesitant, so I took up my camera and let her know that I wanted to take a picture of her when she was sitting down. Finally she sat down and I started to photograph her. The other women in the compartment noticed what was going on and they became quite interested. I took about five photographs of this woman and then I gave my camera to one of the others and asked if she'd take a photo of both of us.

By this time the women had changed their opinion, thinking her honored now for all the attention I was giving her. They opened up their lunch baskets and *began to pass out dosas and fruit to the Muslim woman and me. And after lunch we sang songs for each other, riding together in harmony.*

Later that day, an elderly woman and her daughter appeared in the doorway of our compartment. We had more room now because two of the others had gotten off. I looked around at the faces of those who were left and saw them shake their heads with tight little movements and pursed lips. These were very high caste women I was riding with and they didn't want to be in the company of the backward caste. I hoped they might have learned something from our experience with the Muslim, but years of tradition take their toll. No one moved over to make any room. Finally I got up and took the old woman's hand, leading her to my seat. There was only room for one, so she sat on the floor and leaned on the knees of her daughter who took my seat.

I could never speak to the lower caste women, since we couldn't understand each other's language. So I had to work harder at communicating, be more intimate, make more eye contact. The two women who were now in my seat looked at me with eyes full of gratitude. They bowed their heads and joined their hands, leaning toward me in a gesture of appreciation. I returned the gesture, thankful to them for the chance to be of service. Then I walked down the aisle to the open door, held on tightly to the brass handles and stretched out as far as I could into the humid, monsoon air.

After a while, the woman and her daughter appeared behind me, sitting on a bale of hay across from the open door. I was startled, at first, lost in reverie and continents away in my train of thought. But seeing them there, looking up at me with faint smiles and deep dark eyes, was a joy as precious as my faraway fantasies.

I smiled right back and sat down on the floor, taking the mother's hand in mine. She reached down and touched my face, in a gesture so loving I'll never forget it. The daughter reached out for my other hand, and for a moment in time, we three became one in an intimate bonding. I lost track of everything but the grace of the moment, feeling a radiant glow around our circle. As the train clickety-clacked down the dusty track, we sat there together, holding hands, rubbing palms and touching faces.

At the next stop, they had to leave. They tugged and tugged on my arm, begging me to come to their home. I was so sorry I couldn't, but I needed to be in Delhi by the next day. The train soon pulled out, and I hung out the door waving until they were two small figures in the golden light. When I walked back to my seat, a porter was there with a bottle of Campo-Cola and a huge fresh orange. Gifts, he said, from a mother and her daughter.

— JOURNAL ENTRY

New Delhi and Back Again

After two weeks at Anand Niketan, I left for New Delhi, a twenty-four hour train ride away. Bhai had given me the name of his friend, Babul Lal, who was the director of the Gandhi Peace Foundation. I looked him up when I got to Delhi and he invited me to stay with his wife and family.

They had a one-bedroom apartment and three children, plus two cousins who were visiting from the country. The wife didn't speak any English, but she was very gracious and fed me well. I slept on the floor with the children, lined up like matchsticks in a neat little row.

After I had a day to recover from the grueling train ride, Babul Lal approached me that evening with a proposition. The next day he was taking thirty teenagers from all over the country down to Anand Niketan for a two-week work camp. Since it was meant to be a cultural experience as well, how would I like to accompany them so they would have the benefit of interacting with an American?

"Ride on that train for another twenty-four hours in this ghastly heat? I don't think I could survive, Babul Lal," I said, feeling guilty the minute the words left my lips.

"Well, think about it," he said. "We can get your ticket tomorrow."

By four o'clock the next afternoon, I was on the rails with thirty screaming teenagers, Babul Lal, and Nayan Bala, the mother of one of the teens, who was going along as a chaperone. Nayan Bala, bless her soul, was a college professor who spoke English, and we became fast friends on the journey to Baroda.

The heat was unbearable, the train overcrowded and we picked up more travelers at every stop. Though I was supposed to have a bunk to sleep on, three of us ended up sharing the space. By the time we got to the ashram, two days later, I'd had my fill of crowds and chaos. I went right to my room for a much needed nap, till Nayan Bala arrived with a glass of tea. We started talking and stayed there till dark, sharing pieces of our lives in the flickering light of a kerosene lamp.

She was from the highest caste and had led a fairly privileged life, marrying young and becoming a professional singer of Hindi folk songs.

"Singing was my life," she said. "I loved it more than anything I ever did."

"Do you still sing?" I asked.

"Oh no," she replied. "I had to give it up. When I was twenty-four years old, with three children, my husband died suddenly."

"I don't understand," I said. "Why did that mean you had to give up singing?"

"Because," she explained, "I had to mourn his death. If I continued to sing, people would think I was not mourning."

"But forever? Couldn't you mourn for a year or two, then start singing again?" I asked, "Especially since it was your life?"

"Oh, no," she said, "not here. Maybe in America that would be possible. But here I could not take up singing again. To sing is a sign of being happy. I went back to university to get a degree in teaching. So that is why I am now teaching Hindi."

"But do you *like* that?"

"That is not a question I ask myself. I knew I had to find work and I decided to teach in a university. I did what I needed to do to raise my children. Now they are almost grown and we have managed fine."

Nayan Bala taught me many things in those two weeks, especially the value of hard work, as we labored side by side in the daily work shifts. She was always smiling, no matter how the sweat poured from her brow. At night, we slept out on the roof, our beds side by side so we could talk ourselves to sleep. Occasionally she'd reach over and touch my hand, thanking me for listening to the stories of her life. "Nayan Bala," I'd whisper, "I love you for your sharing. Thank you for giving so much to me." Then we'd drift off to the sound of tribal drums and the whoosh of the breeze in the bamboo leaves.

Since monsoon season is the time of marriages, festivities in the villages went on through the night. One evening Bhai arranged for the tribal teenagers to meet with the youth from the Delhi program. The young Adivasis arrived by bullock cart, beating drums and playing handmade bamboo flutes. Decked out in festive wedding costumes, they gathered in two circles – girls in the middle, boys outside – and began rotating in opposite directions. The drums got faster and louder as the boys worked into a frenzied pace, with the girls, in turn, tightening their circle, their backs to the boys, their arms entwined.

Bridegroom on his
wedding day.

The well-dressed and sophisticated urban boys had never seen anything like this before and their mouths hung open at the sight of their peers in feathers and loincloths, lost in the rapture of tribal dance. Suddenly one let out a whoop and jumped into the circle, dancing the latest steps from Delhi's discos. Then a few more joined and the circle grew, levis and loincloths side by side. Without missing a beat, the tribals backed out and the boys from the city took their place, dancing wildly around the girls.

When the drums finally died down, the teens screamed out in wild applause, howling and hooting in total abandon. Unable to speak each other's language, these two groups of young adults managed to merge two eras in time.

The next morning we were all on a work shift in the field, forty workers in a chain passing buckets of stones from the riverbed to the building site. It went on for hours in the humid monsoon heat and I grew impatient, knowing the job could be done more efficiently with the tractor and wagon.

"This is crazy," I said to Nayan Bala, who had started working long before me. "Why don't we use the machinery here and save ourselves lots of time and effort? It's ridiculous to be passing these little buckets from one person to another, up and down ladders, from the river to the hilltop. It's such a waste of energy."

"We are happy to be contributing to this building," she said. "It is good for people to have work, to know when this barn is finished that they helped put it together. For these children, it is the best lesson that they learn the value of hard work and the joy of working together. For no one here is it a waste of energy." I was too humbled to say anything more, but something about time changed for me that day.

LEFT: Nayan Bala (right) and a student from New Delhi help in the workchain.

FACING PAGE: Four Hindus and an American photographer.

At the end of the two weeks, Nayan Bala and her daughter, Radhika, invited me to stay with them in New Delhi for awhile. I was thrilled to meet the rest of the family and ended up staying for another week.

When we got home one night, three of Nayan Bala's relatives had just arrived from making a sacred pilgrimage to the Ganges River, a trip that all Hindus try to make before they die. They had been on the journey for weeks, traveling hundreds and hundreds of miles by bus in the dreadful heat. Though it was late when they arrived, they sat up till five o'clock sharing the details and drama of their experience, overflowing with excitement and great pride about their accomplishment.

Though I didn't understand a word they were saying, I sat in the room the whole time watching them tell about their spiritual saga. I was lifted up by their energy and thrilled to witness the sharing of such a significant journey.

Before we finally went to bed, they opened up their little bottle of Ganges water and dabbed it on my forehead, eyes and mouth, saying prayers in Hindi as they shared the holy liquid. The next day they dressed me up in a sari and all their jewelry, saying, "If we make you an honorary Hindu, then you ought to look like one."

WHAT'S FAIR IS FAIR – OR IS IT?

One rickshaw driver said he could get me to the Gandhi Foundation for 100 rupees. Another said 75. Another, 50. I went with the last one. He didn't know the way and we ended up on the other side of town, miles away from my destination. After going around in circles, he got out and said, "This will cost you extra – 100 more rupees." "No way," I said. "This is your problem, not mine. It's your fault we're lost, so why should you punish me?" "You must pay more. We have gone farther than I thought," he insisted, flailing his arms. By this time I was out of my seat, flailing my arms right back at him. "I will not pay you more than 50 rupees! And if you don't get on your seat and start pedaling, I will pay you nothing. Nothing! Zero rupees!" I screamed, making huge zeros with my thumbs and forefingers. "Do you understand???"

There I was, in the middle of a busy street, screaming foreign words at this already confused rickshaw driver. But no one seemed to care. Not even the driver. People scream at each other all the time, in all different languages. He was as frustrated as I, but he got back on his seat, his tawny back glistening with sweat in the scorching heat. "What's wrong with me?" I thought, as I crawled back in, exhausted and frustrated. "What's another 50 rupees? Is it really worth screaming at somebody? It'd cost ten times that in New York City. Why can't I just relax?" But no, in India I found my "principles" were forever getting in the way.

The longer I was in India, the better I got at expecting nothing, the less it mattered what was right or wrong. What is, is. What was, was. And eventually it sunk in that there is no right or wrong. There are only the consequences of our behavior. So *what* if to mail a package I had to stand in seven different lines, to be given seven different instructions by seven different people, none of whom really cared if it ever got mailed anyway? So what if it took three hours and twenty-seven minutes to pick up my mail at American Express or half that to buy a can of beans? What was so important about my time that I couldn't spend it standing in line, when Indian citizens manage without complaint? Is there really something about time that can be wasted? What's the big difference between spending time and wasting time? Does my life mean more if I spend time? Less if I waste time? What does time mean anyway? Questions like these came up a lot – until the awesome questionlessness that is India settled into me.

Then I began to relish all my moments, not just those I had assigned to pleasure. I started organizing my life differently, allowing whole days for one task. When I went into the bank to cash a traveler's check, I smiled when I saw twelve people in line, and happily pulled out my latest paperback. I thought it interesting that they didn't have computers or Xeroxes and that every desk was piled high with stacks and stacks of paper.

Once I let go of how I thought things "should be," India became a place of endless entertainment. Unfortunately, it took about six weeks to let go. And being there in the middle of their peak vacation season didn't help matters any.

India is wonderful as long as you have no needs. It's only when you want to get from one place to another that this country takes on the nature of the beast, becoming an impenetrable system with no ears, brain or heart. I feel like I'm trying to get out of a riptide.

I'm supposed to leave for Cairo in two days and when I went for my ticket, they said my agent had left the country for two weeks. There was no ticket or reservation for me.

Nobody is responsible for anything. Life is a huge wave and wherever it washes you up on the shore is the place you were meant to be. Forget control. Forget plans. There is nothing to do but react to what comes your way. And I'm still so unenlightened, I'm furious most of the time.

— JOURNAL ENTRY

I *woke up today feeling that my journey was over. My reasons for being
out here have changed pretty drastically, with a change in perpective from the political to the spiritual. Everything is kind of shifting around inside and I find myself
in a cosmic pause of sorts. Not knowing anything for sure, but open to the remotest of
possibilities, including a return to this land of crusty clay if the spirit so urges.*

*After three months in India, I've come to love her challenges, her curious
customs and constant chaos. I'm beginning to feel at home in the great unknown,
having abandoned illusions of power and control. Huge chunks of righteousness and
self-regard have melted off in the presence of real wisdom and true community, so
manifest in the quiet loving actions of those I've been with. As Emerson said, "When
half-gods go, the gods arrive."*

— JOURNAL ENTRY

Painting a billboard in Alexandria.

EGYPT: NEW FRIENDS IN AN ANCIENT LAND

When I arrived in Cairo, I expected to meet Mr. Charles Hamati, the brother of a man I'd met in Syracuse a few months before I left. A couple had come into the store where I was working, and when I heard them speaking in a foreign language I asked where they were from. Both were Arab Christians who'd been working and researching in Lebanon and were forced to leave when their homes were bombed. George had been a brother in a Catholic order, and his wife, Salwa, a Catholic nun. We had a lot in common and became fast friends in the little time left before my trip.

When I was in Bombay, I received a letter from Salwa about George's death, and the address of his brother Charles, whom she suggested I visit. I wrote to Charles from India, but there was no time for response so I didn't know until I got to Cairo if he'd even received my letter. When I called from the airport, he invited me to his home, and I jumped in a cab when I saw the long lines for the overcrowded buses. For the next two hours, we sat in a traffic jam that made the Los Angeles freeway look like the Indy 500. A few miles and four hours down the road, we came to the street where Charles lived.

He looked just like his brother and had George's photos all around. When I started to talk about meeting George and how special he was in my life, we both cried and grieved together the loss of a brother and friend. Then Charles' wife, Violette, came in with soda and crackers and we all sat down for a friendly visit.

Charles was nearly deaf, but he spoke English well. Violette spoke little English but understood some, and was fluent in French and Arabic. So our conversations went like this: I spoke very loudly to George in English, then he looked to Violette for translation since he's used to reading her lips. She repeated it to him in French, slowly enough for him to read and me to partially understand, so I could correct what I realized she misinterpreted because she didn't understand my English. It took quite a while to get an idea across.

The next day Charles got a gray "Magic Slate," the kind that erases when the cellophane sheet is lifted up. That way we could talk all afternoon, me writing my part, him speaking his.

Violette and Charles were thrilled to have me in their home, begging me to stay longer. It seemed that much was lacking in their own relationship and my presence brought a welcome change of pace to the nagging, nervous energy that usually filled their house. Violette spent hours each day preparing amazing amounts of food for our meals and Charles consumed my every moment with Magic Slate conversations.

Charles and Violette have a son studying at the university in Cairo. They bought him a taxi so he could support himself and drive them around when they needed a ride. He came by regularly to drive us to all the tourist spots. I knew I should have checked into a hotel, since all I really needed was a good rest after India and a chance to be alone. Being in the presence of a man driven to serve me was the last thing I needed.

"Where do you want to go today?" Charles would ask, the moment I walked in.

"Stay here – Read – O.K.?" I'd write on my Magic Slate.

"Oh no, you can't be in Cairo and just read. There are too many things to be seen."

"Too hot for tourist spots," I'd write. "Too much bother for your son."

"My son will do what I say. Today we will go to the pyramids, then the great mosque, and tomorrow, the National Museum."

While he was making all the arrangements, Violette would be cooking up a storm, serving a breakfast of eggs, cheese, bread, hot cereal, cold cuts, fruit, juice and rich, black Egyptian coffee. They kept piling things on my plate, no matter how much I insisted I'd had enough.

Our trip to the pyramids was another ordeal, with two hours spent going less than ten miles. Traffic seemed to always be like that. It never changed. But seeing the Sphinx and the Great Pyramid jutting out from the desert floor, monolithic tributes to an ancient culture, I was ripped from the present and hurled into history.

I climbed into the narrow opening, up and up through the musty corridor until I came at last to the sepulchral chambers. Breathing heavily in the dank surroundings, I touched the stones and smelled the smells, trying to imagine the rituals they conjured to memorialize death in 3000 B.C. Standing in the center of the Great Pyramid was as awesome as climbing into daybreak at Annapurna Sanctuary.

The mountains, as majestic as they are, are part of the natural world and are reckoned with in that perspective, as simple wonders of this amazing earth. But the pyramids, and the massive guardians that stand before them, are meditations on the vastness of human potential. How in the world did they manage to build them? From what kind of consciousness did the people cooperate? Where did all the stones come from? Did people spend whole lifetimes doing nothing else? Who were they worshipping? How are we different now? What's changed for humanity?

In a few days in Cairo, we had visited the magnificent National Museum with King Tut and all his entourage, the largest mosque in Egypt, the Sphinx and the pyramids, the marketplace, the Capitol buildings and the great Mother Nile. I was exhausted and Charles was full of newfound energy. I tried to talk to Violette about needing a break, but she said it was impossible to change Charles's mind – and he had it made up to be my tour guide.

When I entered Egypt I was required to cash $150 into Egyptian money, no matter how short my visit would be. That was more than I spent in a month in India. Charles wouldn't let me spend a cent, so I decided to take an overnight trip to Alexandria and splurge on a nice hotel room. I found a beautiful room for $26, with the first bathtub I'd seen since Hong Kong. And it wasn't even down the hall.

I took a luxurious bubble bath, then lounged around my room in their huge plush towels, feeling like I could identify with the phrase "the idle rich." What freedom to be all by myself, with nowhere to go, no one to talk to, in a hotel room that had running water, a desk and a full-length mirror. The ceilings and doors were very high and I felt like Loretta Young every time I swept in. I hadn't seen myself reflected in many months, and my image in the mirror was quite a surprise. The months of sickness and hardship had taken their toll, etching new creases across my brow and leaving me twenty pounds lighter. My clothes were all baggy, but I put on the brightest outfit I had and and went out in search of an elegant restaurant.

Discovering that I wasn't good at spending money, I settled for a decent Greek restaurant, splurged on a fancy cocktail and baklava for dessert and went home early to make tapes and write letters. After finding the Mediterranean Sea too dirty to swim in, I decided to head back to Cairo and make plans for Israel.

The next afternoon I pulled into the train station and walked across the street to where Charles and Violette lived. They were thrilled to see me and Violette went straight to the kitchen to cook up something while Charles looked around for the Magic Slate. I wrote that I'd be leaving the next day for Tel Aviv and he was heartbroken, pleading with me to stay a few more weeks.

After dinner, I went into the kitchen. "Violette, please don't make anything for me tomorrow. I fast every Friday from eight to eight, so I don't need food for my trip, and I have too much to carry anyway." "You must take something with you," she insisted. "No, really, I mean it. I'll just give it away. I don't eat on Friday," I repeated. "Just a little something," she said. "It's a long ride to Tel Aviv."

The next morning sitting on the dining room table for me to take were one whole chicken, one dozen hard boiled eggs, one quart of homemade pickles, one pound of Egyptian bologna, five round tins of cheese, eight chocolate candy bars, a litre of tangerine juice and throat lozenges.

Charles had to follow me onto the bus carrying all the food. I started handing it out after a couple of hours and by the time we reached the border I was the most popular passenger on the bus. And the messiest. When I broke my fast at eight o'clock, all that was left were two hard boiled eggs and a few triangles of cheese.

97

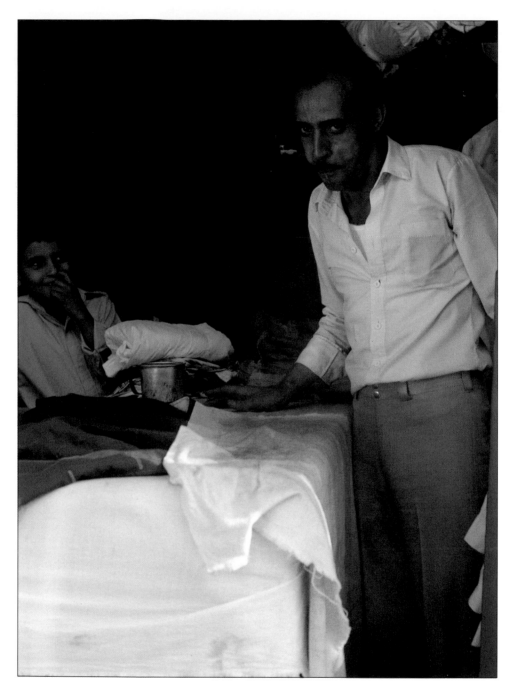

He set up his ironing board in a little garage and took in clothes to press for a business.
He didn't have a steam iron, so he took a big gulp of water, then sprayed it out in a
fine mist over the clothes. I laughed so hard when I saw him, he did it over and over
again just to keep me there. By the time I left, most of the clothes were saturated.

The scenario here is something else. Charles and Violette think I was sent by God and treat me like some kind of saint. They think the Muslims are gaining control of the world and have established that my mission is to counteract that force wherever I go. Schools should force children to study religion, they think.

Charles has fallen in love with me, in a very gentlemanly and grandfatherly way, and he keeps insisting that there are no people in his life who care as much as I do about his feelings and ideas. As if I'm some kind of angel of mercy who's come to rescue him from his grief and grievances, he tells me over and over in Egyptian dramatics how important it is that I stay longer in Cairo, forever if possible.

There was a time in my life when I would have eaten up this kind of attention, but I am wearied and saddened by it now. To think that people are so isolated, have spent whole lifetimes without a sense of commonness with anyone. He's so fanatically Christian, yet hasn't found Christ in anyone but me. Why don't we look *at each other?*

I wonder how it is that I can go from one strange place to another and always find open and loving people, when some people live in the same neighborhood, go to the same church for thirty years and still say that no one there has a heart. How can we miss the point of our lives like that?

— JOURNAL ENTRY

It's way past midnight, but it's like rush hour on the streets below. The honking is incredible. When I tried to play my guitar, even with the windows shut, there was so much noise I couldn't hear to tune it. Do not forget this. I think it's why there's so much trouble in the Middle East. There is no potential for peace in the midst of this kind of chaos.

A lot of emotions come up when I move from one country to another. I'm at odds with the new, lonely for the old. The changes tend to send me inward, to my longings for home, comfort, someone familiar. I want someone to hold me and rub my head, and tell me it's O.K. to feel weary and alone.

After ten days in Cairo, I'm ready for a transfer — homesick for India, but heading for Israel. The frenzied bustle is a bit too much and I'm sick of getting writer's cramp from talking about Christianity. Believers should just live it and stop talking so much about it. Islam is not the enemy. The enemy, in fact, is not even outside us. It's this imaginary line we've drawn down the middle of our foreheads, so that right can live on one side and wrong on the other. That's the enemy. That kind of smugness and ignorance.

The place of transformation is at the interface of opposites. It's at this point of convergence that reconciliation can occur. So why, then, do we repel our opposites? Why arm ourselves against the forces that can be our liberation if we would only dance with them? Only new life could come from the merging of worldwide faiths. Only new possibilities could evolve out of a mingling of east and west, communism and capitalism, militaries and peace corps. But we hold it, instead, like there is dark and light, like what is not of us is of the dark, while we ourselves contain the night that we send our sons to fight.

Charles talks about nobody having a heart anymore while his own is so clenched he can hardly breathe, afraid if he gives love away it will not come back. Our military stance is to not back down, to not reduce arms until the enemy reduces first. And our enemy takes the same stance. And Charles's neighbors take the same stance. And life on earth begins to die.

Where do we learn such things? Where do we learn to wait for someone else to take the risk, to open the heart? Why doesn't someone start telling the truth, that it's at the perilous edge of risk itself that the energy comes to transform our lives?

— JOURNAL ENTRY

Cairo, Egypt.

Akko, Israel.

ISRAEL: THE HOLY LAND?

Arriving in Tel Aviv was, in an odd kind of way, like coming home. All my life I'd dreamed of going to Israel, being in the Holy Land of mysteries and miracles. Though I was raised a Christian, in some deep down place I felt a Jew. When I first heard of the Holocaust, the horror and terror of that event had more impact on my spirit than anything I'd ever known or felt.

Having grown up feeling different from the others – confused about my emotions, alienated from my family, discriminated against by my Church – I knew in my bones a sense of exile. When I had studied Judaism in the novitiate, something about that trust in Yahweh through the desert called me by name. In some powerful way, Israel was in me long before I got to her.

After the ancient and Arab Egypt, I was surprised to find such a westernized city, with all the modern comforts of home. The military presence was overwhelming, with heavily armed soldiers everywhere. I spent the first few days wandering around, swimming in the Mediterranean and enjoying my solitude. From there I headed to Akko, an old Crusaders' stronghold a few hours up the coast.

I had the address of Wagia Zand-Irani, a British-trained museum guard at the old city museum. I'd been given his name by Amos Mund, a man from Berlin who had sent me twelve annotated pages of names and addresses of people working for justice in fifteen different countries. Amos had lived in Israel many years, studying Hebrew and working with Palestinian Arab villagers in Galilee. He sent me his list of friends when he saw an ad I put in *Sojourners* magazine requesting addresses of kindred spirits around the world. Wagia Zand-Irani, a Greek Catholic, was one such person.

When I got off the bus, a tall young man came up to greet me.

"Hello, what's your name?" he said.

"Jan, what's yours?" I replied.

"Yosef. Where are you going? I'll take you there."

"To the old museum. I'm looking for Mr. Zand-Irani."

"But first, come here," he said, taking my hand and leading me up some old steps.

I took my hand away and asked where he was heading.

"To the top of this hill – from there we can see all the ruins. It's my favorite place," he said, taking my hand again.

"Yosef, I don't want to walk up all these steps. I'm trying to find the old museum. And stop grabbing my hand."

"But you will love this. I promise," and up we walked, as if I'd never taken a course in assertiveness training.

He was right, it was a beautiful spot. But his constant advances became very annoying.

"Yosef, I'm not interested in a relationship with you and you're making me angry.

Now I'm going back and I'd rather be alone," I said starting down the ancient stone stairway.

He bolted after me, grabbing my hand and pulling me along behind him. "This is such fun," he laughed, like we were a happy couple in a Salem commercial. "I'm so glad you've come to my city. Tonight we will go dancing."

"No way!" I thought. "If I'm lucky, I'll never see you again."

He led me over to the old museum, where I found Mr. Zand-Irani and explained who I was. The old man was delighted to meet me and took me on a grand tour of the thirteenth-century Crusaders' fortress, through the catacombs, underground tunnels and endless secret chambers. When we were done, we went to his home where I met his wife and several children, some of whom had brought their children home to visit.

We had dinner together and I mentioned the character Yosef, who'd met me at the bus. From his description, they knew who he was.

"His name is not Yosef," said one of the sons. "His name is Ali Amir."

"Why would he tell me that then?" I asked.

"He's Arab, but he would not give you his Arab name, thinking you would judge him badly. If you thought he was Israeli, he would have a better chance."

"Whether one is Arab or Israeli doesn't matter," I said. "What's important is that they respect my privacy and take me seriously when I say I want to be alone."

"When you are here, Arab or Israeli is the only thing that matters," he said, and the others nodded in agreement as they downed their yoghurt and falafels. The father said it was not good to be talking like that and quickly changed the subject.

Since the Zand-Irani home was quite crowded, I spent the night in a hostel a few blocks away, where I had to fight off the manager, who was determined to share my bed. Between Yosef and this man, I was physically and psychically exhausted from protecting my space, and took the first bus out of town the next morning, ending up at the Sea of Galilee.

There were A-frame cabins for twelve dollars a night, right on the edge of the famous sea. But again I was harassed by an insistant manager eager to inflict his company on me and unwilling to respect my need for privacy. That night on the Sea of Galilee I wondered if it wasn't as much a miracle to walk through the twentieth century as a forgiving and loving person as it was to walk on water in the year 30 A.D.

Drawn toward the Wailing Wall with the need to mourn, I made my way to Jerusalem as soon as I could. Leaving all my gear in the bus station, I went to the old city in search of the wall, and was soon approached by a man who wondered where I was going.

"To the Wailing Wall," I told him, without looking right or left.

"Come with me, I'll show you where it is," he offered.

"I don't need any help. I can find it on my own," I said, making my way through the narrow, winding streets of old Jerusalem.

He wouldn't leave and kept insisting I follow him to the Wall. My little voice said,

"This man didn't do anything to hurt you. Maybe he really wants to help you. Why don't you give him a chance? It's not fair to punish him because of what others have done."

"O.K." I said. "I'll follow you to the Wall. Where is it?"

He reached for my hand and I pulled away, "Let's just walk."

We went up and down hundreds of stairs, through alleys, in and out of shopping areas, then we stopped for a soda which he graciously bought.

"Are we almost there?" I asked.

"Almost," he said, taking my hand and holding it tightly.

I shouted for him to let go of my hand, then I finally shook it loose and turned to leave. I walked on alone for a few more blocks, coming to the top of a hill overlooking the great Wailing Wall. Too weary to go down, I sat on the edge, watching the men in black bow and pray, my own body bent in mournful prayer. Whatever became of the Holy Land?

Old Library in Jerusalem.

There is so much tension in the Middle East, manifesting itself as a kind of deafness, an aggressive coldheartedness — no one will hear the other's needs. I stayed with Jews and Arabs, Muslims and Christians, each having assimilated to some degree the propaganda that stifles human kindness. They all treated me royally, but could not find it in their hearts to accommodate one another.

I've been in Israel two weeks and can't quite get connected, leaving one place after another to deflect the harassment of men who think they're the answer to my prayers. Just arrived in Jerusalem where I came to a convent guest house for retreat, not knowing what else to do to bring my parts together. A good cry, I'm sure, would release this pain, but I can't seem to loosen the knots around my heart.

On the way here I stopped in Nazareth, thinking I might stay awhile. But the streets were teeming with tourists with cameras, clicking away at huge structures built over the site of Joseph's carpentry shop and the place where the Annunciation supposedly occurred. I went into the chapel to light some candles and find some peace, but the groups kept whizzing by, catching photos on the run, as the tour guide prodded them along to the postcard and trinket booths. The merchants are still in the temple.

The Holy Land seems such an odd place for a crisis of faith. I swam last week in the same water that Jesus walked on, collecting little stones to carry with me and help me remember — like the Hindus with their Ganges water — but the magic, the mystery is outside my grasp and I hardly remember what it's like to believe. It feels like all my supports have crumbled and it is I, alone, who must power myself on with what little energy I have left.

Before, when people would say what courage it took to be making this trip, I never knew what they meant, I was so lifted up by some guiding force that led me from one communion to another. Now, in this darkness, it is clear what they meant and I can only say I have no courage — I am afraid, filled with the night, with the sorrow of my heart reverberating in its chambers like an echoing wail. I feel on the bottom rung of the lowest ladder, humbled by what seems a terrible fall from grace.

Oh God, may I not lose heart on this journey....

— JOURNAL ENTRY

GREECE: A GIFT TO THE SPIRIT

I left the port of Haifa on a boat bound for Athens, where I'd be meeting my mother in two weeks. I hadn't seen her in over a year and she was coming to travel with me for six weeks through Europe. At the age of sixty-one, she bought herself a backpack, a good pair of hiking shoes and a copy of *Europe on $25 a Day*. Then she practiced walking around her neighborhood with her pack on her back to get in shape for the adventure. The thought of working and playing in Europe with my mom at my side was so exciting I could hardly stand the two-week wait.

With time on my hands, I took a trip to Lesbos, a beautiful island which was the birthplace of Sappho, a poet and teacher who flourished on the isle around 600 B.C. She was celebrated as one of Greece's most passionate and profound poets, but her work was destroyed by early Christian patriarchs. I took a bus to Eressos, the village where she was born, hoping to find some memorial or tribute, but found nothing there that stood in her honor.

I took photographs today with the soul of me engaged in the seeing for the first time since India. I took the easy things first — the rocks, the sea, the towering cliffs — wanting to people the scene but having no one near. On the way back to my room, I found two women, Maggie and Carla from Holland and England, who had set up camp on the sandy beach. I asked if I could photograph them tomorrow and they said no, they were too shy. Then I shared my experiences of the last few weeks and told them how much I needed to be with them for healing and comfort. They understood immediately and changed their minds, saying I could photograph them all I wanted if it would ease my pain.

— Journal entry

Mom and I had our own little Mass on Sunday morning — bread, wine, grapes, flowers, even my guitar, so I sang her birthday song for the offertory. We didn't have a Bible so we each talked about our favorite passage and why it was important to us. And for communion we shared experiences about feeling close to people even though we were far away. We both cried during the whole thing, so full of joy at the wonders of our lives....

We've been spending most our time on the beach reading, talking, sleeping and being quiet together. The other day when she was taking a nap, I made a huge checkerboard in the sand, then went snorkeling for the checkers. I found twelve round white rocks and twelve round black ones, so when she woke up, the board was all set. We played three games and she won them all.

— JOURNAL ENTRY

Theo, a farmer from the island Antiparos.

Gardener in East Germany.

A New Perspective on Making Change

My peace work changed dimensions once I arrived in Europe and returned to Western civilization. Suddenly the Eastern approach – *life is perfect as it is being unveiled to you, so do not be concerned with changing it; seek only to accept it* – was upstaged by an attitude of industrious activism where people with a social conscience spent entire lifetimes trying to change things. The shift in perspective was radical and took some getting used to after several months of immersion in a culture where justice was something meted out by the gods in a cosmic gesture of karmic balance.

I met with peace groups in Naples and Rome and was surprised at their interests in China and the Philippines, finding, as I answered their questions on the political situation in these countries, that I really wanted to be talking about India and how being there transformed my faith and politics.

I wasn't the same peace activist who left New York sixteen months earlier, full of information I wanted to share. Spending time with people from different cultures taught me to listen, to sit with and learn from the silence as well as the speaking. My feelings and thoughts, which I once thought of as reactions to events, started to appear as the source of events, confirming the belief that our lives are as we imagine them to be.

It took every resource in my entire being to cope with a culture that was the polar opposite of my own, but something powerful was born of the union of those opposites. It happens that way in the brain, when both hemispheres combine forces and new thought is created. After many months, when I finally understood that nothing new can evolve without the merging of opposites, life itself became another kind of challenge. I came back to the West wondering not what to *do* about life, but how to *be* in it more fully.

Though my roots would always be Christian, my limbs were shooting out in all directions, touching and being touched by the all-pervasive Spirit of the Universe. The idea of one personal God seemed insufficient after having so many gods and goddesses to connect with for so long. I had no doctrine I was attached to, no particular beliefs that separated me from anyone, anywhere. All I knew was that in some mysterious way, I was profoundly a part of all living beings. Besides God's face, I saw my own reflection in the face of my neighbors, and felt their joy and grief as if it were mine.

Behind what I felt and thought, behind what I knew and aspired to, I was beginning to find who I was. And, even more important, to accept that I would be that person forever, contradictions and all. When I stopped trying to change myself, I stopped trying to change anyone else, and peace became the life force that moved me along. This was the person who arrived in Germany to meet with activists, speak about peace and photograph the massive demonstrations that were going on throughout the country.

I finally made it to Berlin and met Amos, whose friends I had visited all over the world thanks to the addresses he sent me before I left. He was a wonderful man who looked like a blend of Karl Marx and Santa Claus, with the mind of Marx and the generosity of Santa.

Amos was active in the Christian Peace Movement as well as the Communist Party, seeing himself as a bridge between the two. What he found difficult was the shortsightedness of each group and their lack of tolerance for each other. "The solutions to our problems will come after we carefully analyze each situation." he said. "Idealism is not effective. In fact, it's a deterrent. It doesn't work to force goals or to squeeze present realities into certain ideologies. What I'm working for is to end the exploitation of people, and my work in the Communist Party is a step in that direction. I hope to be able to help Christians analyze better and to help my comrades in the party see the connections between the two groups." A biblical scholar and political analyst, Amos was a great companion and stimulating conversationalist who introduced me to many friends on both sides of the Iron Curtain.

We went to a small village in East Germany to visit a friend of his who was pastor of the local church. She served a tiny congregation that met weekly in the parsonage in a small room that had been converted into a chapel. The pastor said that she believed in the ideals of socialism and had no trouble reconciling them with Christianity. To her, the ultimate goals of each were to ensure that everyone's needs were taken care of. At one point she tried to join the Communist party but was not allowed to, because she was a Christian pastor.

She said that the role of communism is to analyze the problems, to see what is wrong, not to idealize about solutions. "Socialism is essentially very attractive, meeting the basic needs of every citizen. That's why capitalist states cannot aford to leave it alone and let it work. It's too threatening to their profits. We understand that no good theory was ever put into practice with violence and oppression. That's why the hard work is upon us of creating a way of instituting its principles in a democratic manner. Russia's mistakes are very serious, but so, too, are those of the United States."

My friend Amos of Berlin.

We just returned from the concentration camp at Dachau, where 32,000 people died as a result of disease, malnutrition and physical oppression. I had visited there in 1972 and found it very different this time. They're showing a different film now, with much less actual footage, that makes it easier to bear. They're also claiming that the gas chambers were never used in Dachau and the gas rooms are all cleaned up and freshly painted. What I remember from 1972 are the terrible scratches in the wall where people were lined up for showers and found out they were getting gassed instead. They tore their fingernails into the wooden walls in their last attempt at making an imprint or clinging to life. That image was so embedded in my memory, and now they tell me it never happened.

That the Holocaust occurred is an outrage huge enough to bring us all to our knees. That there are now revisionists trying to rewrite this episode of human history, changing the facts to diminish our guilt, is as evil and unforgivable as the Holocaust itself.

— JOURNAL ENTRY

A Brief Retreat in Utrecht

Just coming back to reality after a few days' retreat in a cozy little room here — a health resort for the soul, compliments of a friend of a friend who runs a psychic institute in this lively little city of Utrecht. I spent two days in bed, recovering from a mad dash through northern Germany with too many commitments and too many nights in cold, strange bedrooms. Now I'm moving very slowly to discover what's going on in this area that feels life-giving and hopeful.

There is a demonstration in Amsterdam that I hope to attend tomorrow. Older women from the area are demonstrating in front of Queen Beatrix's palace, appealing to her as a fellow senior citizen to think of the future and sign a bill keeping Cruise and Pershing missiles out of the Netherlands. After the drab and very serious demonstrations of Germany, I'm looking forward to something a little spunkier from the Dutch.

— Journal entry

ABOVE & FACING PAGE: Peace demonstration in Amsterdam, The Netherlands.

I get so caught up in dialogue and action when I'm on the road, always involved in the ultimate questions, the endless movement with others who are tying to understand and articulate what's going on, what went on and what may come to pass. I'm trying to learn the balance that works for me, to resolve the question of what I owe to myself, so that I stay replenished, and what I owe to the whole. I've gotten better at it in the past year, knowing that I'll never contribute anything to peace if it doesn't live like a force within me.

I've had incredible encounters with many people here — as intimate as we can be as immediately as possible since time is always at a premium. The goings are difficult, filling my hours on the train with a rare kind of nostalgia. I'm ready to get off. To take my rest. To go into a room that is not someone else's and close the doors, cry out this accumulation of grief, need, awareness. I've been too long in the Museum of People's History.

Now I need a room with nothing but a candle. No books because I can't resist reading them. No people because I can't resist loving them. Just a simple light and some silence, so I can tell this story to myself. So I can begin to understand what has happened since the road has been my home.

— FROM A LETTER HOME

EAST MEETS WEST:
AN INTERVIEW WITH A FELLOW PEACEMAKER

Someone in Utrecht told me about a man from India walking around the world for peace. He'd just arrived in Amsterdam, so I arranged to meet him after a presentation he was making in a church. I was very much looking forward to it, imagining all we'd have in common, anxious to hear his stories and share some of mine. When we finally sat down to talk, it felt like the classic merging of two civilizations.

Prem Kamur had been traveling for a year and a half, carrying only a small pack and no money. He did not use public transportation and only walked to his destinations. For food and lodging, he relied on the kindness of people on the road, and if there were no people to provide for him, then he went without food.

I, on the other hand, Miss Media Queen from the West, had my pack so loaded with technology I could hardly lift it. Besides that, I also carried a guitar and a camera bag. I never went without food, except on Friday when I fasted, and I used public transportation whenever I could.

Though we differed in externals, the intent and experience of our journeys were much the same. Here are some excerpts from an interview with him in Amsterdam:

JP: What are you hoping to achieve through your journey?

PK: My intention is to contact and communicate with people. I think people of different nations have little or no communication, and after traveling for a year and a half, I am convinced that the information we do have is deviated and slanted for some purpose that serves the interest of a few. I believe that personal contact is a necessity when people are trying to gather information and discuss new ideas about solving problems.

JP: What insights have you gained?

PK: I have not spent a single penny on this trip and it is clear I am totally dependent on others. I have found that I get what I need without asking. This never happened before.

Another thing is that there are always people there to take care of you as long as your mission is selfless. I believe there is a Supreme Power that exists and in His domain everything is coordinated. We are never the best coordinators. This walk has made me totally fearless. I am not afraid of anything, not even death.

JP: I've noticed a kind of merging between people of political orientation and those with a more spiritual orientation. We seem to be bridging that gap in a way that has not happened in our history that I know of. Have you experienced that in your travels?

PK: I think that the day philosophy and physics departed from each other, the whole problem started. The head goes in one direction, the heart in another. The most balanced people I have met are those who have found a harmony between what their heart has to say and what their head has to say.

JP: What do you think most people are seeking?

PK: Change, I think. They know there is something wrong and they are searching for a right way of living. If anything is difficult, it is the spiritual path. I compare it to going to the summit of Mt. Everest. When you are at base camp, the going is much easier. As you go farther, the more difficult the going becomes. You make one step forward and two steps back. It is not so easy, but once you attain it, you realize the happiness you gain out of it.

Many people want to retain everything they possess, to have a luxurious life and still experience the benefits of the other side. We have not achieved the combination between the two. Whatever we do – whether we go to the North Pole or the South Pole – we decide either to go north or south. If we decide to go, it means we go the whole way. A lot of people are not prepared for that. They don't want to make real change.

The difficulty I am finding now is that there is a spirit among people to dominate nature, dominate the universe. We try to find one solution and create three more problems. Every system in nature recycles but our own. We are dumping on this earth a lot of things that will not break down. They are a burden to the earth and will eventually cause the destruction of humankind. We must learn to co-exist with nature. We must accept that plants and animals have an equally important role. With this realization we can change the whole mentality and attitude of our lives.

Another thing I found on my walk is that my main supporters are women. I have a feeling that if we are to see the twenty-first century, it will be an age of spiritualism, solar energy and women. There is a three-thousand-year-old saying that any society that doesn't respect its women or its forests will itself be destroyed. I believe that is true.

Prem Kamur.

U.S. Air Force Base in Greenham Common.

THE ENCAMPMENT AT GREENHAM

Arriving in England brought a mix of many emotions, marking the end of one journey and the beginning of another. Part of me was happy it was coming to an end. I'd taken in so much. Given out so much. And I needed a chance to digest what had happened over all those months.

As I'd lived it out, the day-to-dayness of it felt very casual and ordinary, the pains and privileges of being on the road the same as any other traveller might experience. But when I reflected on the journey as a whole, I sensed its powerful impact in every part of my being.

I spent five days at the U.S. Air Force Base in Greenham Common, where 96 Cruise missiles – NATO's nuclear weapons – were being deployed. Since 1981, hundreds of women from around the world have kept constant vigil at the eight main gates of the air base, in nonviolent protest against these and all nuclear weapons. Some of their direct protest actions have included the takeover of a guard sentry box inside the base where women took control of the public address system, a sit-in at Parliament that forced an open debate of the Cruise issue, and several raids of the base which publicly exposed nuclear missile silos previously hidden and denied by the U.S. military. On December 12, 1982, 30,000 women, men and children from all over Europe linked arms around the nine-mile perimeter to completely "embrace" the base.

While I was there, it rained every day. We slept under plastic tarps thrown across clothesline strung between trees. No one had dry clothes or shoes to wear. There was one smoky wood fire to gather round for warmth and comfort. Every morning by 8:00 A.M., the garbage truck would arrive and all possessions that weren't locked in someone's car would be taken and destroyed by the county workers hired to clear the area. Then they would douse the fire and destroy the bales of hay that were all we had to sit on.

Around dinnertime, a car usually arrived carrying pots of stew and loaves of bread, but there were days when food never arrived. There was nothing easy or predictable about being at Greenham Common. From morning through the night, women sat by the fire singing, strategizing, mothering children, praying, sharing stories and working together.

Trials were going on while I was there and I accompanied twelve women who were being tried for entering the base and splashing paint on several military vehicles. One woman who was being tried was a Presbyterian minister. After they read her charges, she had only one remark: "Yes, I am guilty for putting red paint on those vehicles of death. But in my heart I only feel guilt for using red paint instead of real blood to symbolize the tragedy of these times."

Living on the brink between today and tomorrow, I base my actions as much on hope as on what I know of reality. In my mind, there are two worlds — the one I know, and the one I believe could be true. I strain in every way to make a bridge, knowing we are better than we appear to be. I have no doubt. We're very close to the edge of discovery, very close to touching what we know to be true. We just need time.

That's why the resistance to war. War will take our time from us. So that's where my heart is, caught up in the struggle to hold back the night until we have a chance to make something of our evolution.

— Journal entry

To you women out there
who have taken your lives
and your longings to the common land,
who have dared to make camp
on the shadow's edge,
trading comfort for the nightwatch chill
to speak the resistance
of a hundred thousand lovers
to the theft of our dreams:
the light of your fire is all around us.

To you women out there
who are rending the fences
of danger and delusion,
bending like grass against a bitter wind
to tend the flame for those to come:
we hear the songs that you are singing,
the sound of your hope,
as you weave through the cold metal wire
the ribbons and colors of our lives.

We are the lovers, the dreamers,
the bearers of those to come
who will bear no more the shame of these arms.
We are the hundred thousand squared
warriors of a new age
converged in a circle
preparing new rites
for the passage of peace.
Blessed be, blessed be....

– In honor of all women who are keeping vigil at
military bases around the world.

I left the Women's Peace Encampment at Greenham Common grateful for the chance to have taken my turn at the night watch. Through the early gray mist, I walked quietly to town and boarded a bus to London, wrapped in silence for the two-hour ride. My journey was over.

Once in London, I packed my bags and readied for the flight back to Syracuse, New York. Though I'd come to love the winding road and all its rites of passage, I yearned, as well, for the comforts of home and familiar, loving faces. Somewhere over the Atlantic, I looked out and waved goodbye to all the kind souls who had changed my life, who'd filled my cup and warmed my heart. I needn't weep, for there was no loss; what love they had given, I could keep forever.

Widow on Lesbos, Greece.